Association System of the European Community

Jacqueline D. Matthews

Association System of the European Community

PRAEGER SPECIAL STUDIES IN INTERNATIONAL BUSINESS, FINANCE, AND TRADE

Praeger Publishers   New York   Washington   London

Library of Congress Cataloging in Publication Data

Matthews, Jacqueline D.
    Association system of the European community.

    (Praeger special studies in international business,
finance, and trade)
    Bibliography: p. 156
    Includes index.
    1. European Economic Community. 2. European
Economic Community—Africa. I. Title.
HC241.2.M29   382'.9142   76-12865
ISBN 0-275-23270-0

PRAEGER PUBLISHERS
111 Fourth Avenue, New York, N.Y. 10003, U.S.A.

Published in the United States of America in 1977
by Praeger Publishers, Inc.

Printed in the United States of America

To Marc, Alan, and Colin

PREFACE

This book is based on a doctoral thesis presented to the University of Natal, Durban, South Africa, in December 1974. The initial study was revised to incorporate the Lomé Convention of 1975 and statistics have been updated. Theoretical sections, unsuitable for a wider audience, were curtailed or omitted but the main findings are identical.

With regard to terminology, the European Economic Community is also referred to as the Common Market, the European Community, the Community, or the EEC. The term "Association" refers to the Association System of the EEC, as described in Chapter 2. Since the Lomé Convention, there has been a tendency to drop the name Association but it is retained here for two reasons. First, the alternatives that have been used (solidarity, cooperation, pattern for friendship) are inadequate to describe the special relationship between the EEC and certain countries. Second, the term Association has been used for almost 20 years and the use of an alternative would imply a change in the nature of the relationship between the EEC and those countries, which is not the case.

It should be kept in mind that the Association System is essentially dynamic and that this publication does not include changes that have occurred since January 1, 1976.

ACKNOWLEDGMENTS

I should like to express my thanks to the Human Sciences Research Council, Pretoria, for their financial assistance in the course of this research. The bursary I was awarded in 1971 enabled me to spend three months studying aspects of the European Economic Community at the Institut Européen des Hautes Etudes Internationales at the University of Nice, France; to undertake research at the headquarters of the General Agreement on Tariffs and Trade (GATT) and of the United Nations Conference on Trade and Development (UNCTAD), Geneva; to attend a conference on prospects for integration in the 1970s at the University of Reading, England; and to take part in a study tour of the EEC and other international institutions in the Hague, Brussels, Luxembourg, Strasbourg, and Basel.

Although I am solely responsible for the opinions expressed in this book, I am grateful to those who helped me by discussing the problems under consideration, notably Mr. Groome and Mr. Maggio of the GATT, Mr. Millwood of UNCTAD, professors Etienne, Preiswerk, and Curzon of the Graduate Institute of International Studies, Geneva, Mr. Paul Taylor of the London School of Economics, and Miss Susan Strange of the Royal Institute of International Affairs, London.

I express my appreciation to my supervisors, professors T. van Waasdijk and G. J. Trotter, and especially to my colleague Mr. I. K. Allan, for their critical reading of the manuscript, and to Mrs. D. Hosken for typing the final copy.

Finally, I should like to thank my husband, Peter Matthews, Professor of Geology at the University of Natal, for his help and encouragement throughout the preparation of this work.

CONTENTS

LIST OF TABLES AND MAP

LIST OF ABBREVIATIONS

AAMS	Association of African and Malagasy States
ACP	Africa, Caribbean and Pacific associates
BSL	Botswana, Swaziland, Lesotho
CAP	Common agricultural policy
CET	Common external tariff
COMECON	Council for Mutual Economic Assistance
ECSC	European Coal and Steel Community
EEC	European Economic Community
EFTA	European Free Trade Association
GATT	General Agreement on Tariffs and Trade
GSP	Generalized Scheme of Preferences
ITO	International Trade Organization
LAFTA	Latin American Free Trade Area
LDC	Less-developed countries
MFN	Most-favored nation
OECD	Organization for Economic Cooperation and Development
OEEC	Organization for European Economic Cooperation
UDEAC	Union Douaniére et Economique de l'Afrique Centrale
UNCTAD	United Nations Conference on Trade and Development

In March 1957, six European countries embarked upon a momentous course that is leading them toward economic integration and may eventually link them politically: France, West Germany, Italy, Belgium, the Netherlands, and Luxembourg signed the Treaty of Rome, establishing the European Economic Community (EEC). In January 1973, Britain, Ireland, and Denmark joined the Common Market, thus increasing the Community to nine members.

Although the arduous process of integration and the concomitant changes in internal relations are the important aspects of this venture for members of the Community, countries remaining outside the EEC are more concerned with the external policies of the Common Market. A prominent aspect of these external relations is the Association System, which describes the complex network of agreements between a number of countries and the EEC. Thus, the Association System will be taken here in its broadest sense, to include not only associated states but also countries that have entered into simple trade agreements with the EEC.*

The central theme of this book is to consider the impact of the Association System of the European Economic Community on international trade policies. The basis for Association resides in Articles 131–36 of the Treaty of Rome.† The original purpose of these provisions was to deal with the problem of the relationship between members of the Common Market and their colonies. Full application of the terms of the Rome Treaty to those dependencies was rejected by some members, but a compromise was reached in the concept of Association between the EEC and dependencies.

The most important aspect of the Association was the creation of a free-trade area between the EEC and associates, giving preferential access to exports from both groups into the markets of the other. In addition, financial aid was to be provided to the dependencies for economic and social projects through a European Development Fund, to which all members of the EEC were committed to contribute. Underlying these economic factors was the political aim of maintaining close links between the Western world and African countries on the brink of independence, especially in view of the fact that some EEC members had large investments in those territories.

In 1963, a new type of Association was entered into between the EEC and 18 independent African countries, and more recently, the Lomé Convention

---

*See Map 1.
†See Appendix A for relevant articles of the Rome Treaty, 1957.

of 1975 linked the enlarged Community and 46 African, Caribbean, and Pacific States. Other agreements establishing special forms of association or dealing only with commercial relations have contributed to the variety and complexity of the Association System.

The focus of this work is Africa. Although the EEC has entered into agreements with countries in Europe and other parts of the world, the core of the Association System has always been Africa. Furthermore, the latest agreement—the Lomé Convention—has doubled the number of African associates, and by bringing together ex-French territories and Commonwealth countries, this is leading to a salutary blurring of the old historical division between Francophone and Anglophone Africa. Thus the Association has become a vehicle for African unity. It seems only a matter of time before the whole continent establishes trade and aid links with the European Community, with the exception of the Republic of South Africa. The enlargement of the Community and the extension of the Association affect South Africa's external trade relationships, but for economic and political reasons, the South African Republic is unlikely to become an associate of the EEC.

Apart from its effect on Africa, the Association System has had an impact on wider aspects of international trade. Since its inception, the Association has been criticized by third countries* because it was argued, inter alia, that it would damage the external trade of nonassociates, especially developing countries. It was also maintained that the terms of association and trade agreements were in conflict with the rules of the General Agreement on Tariffs and Trade (GATT). Nevertheless, preferences given to associates have intensified the search of other developing countries for tariff concessions in markets of developed nations. This has resulted in the establishment of the Generalized Scheme of Preferences (GSP), which in turn has contributed to the downfall of the principle of nondiscrimination.

Controversies regarding external relations of the EEC stem from basic disagreements between nations as to the role and function of international trade. Differences of opinion in this respect will persist as long as countries differ in economic structure, patterns of trade, and development.

Our purpose is therefore to examine the impact of Association on these various aspects of international economics. It is beyond the scope of this book to examine whether the Association has fulfilled—or is likely to fulfill—the purpose mentioned in Article 131 of the Treaty of Rome, that is, to promote the economic and social development of the associates. Nor are we concerned with the question of whether foreign trade or economic integration are beneficial or detrimental to developing nations. We accept as a fact that most of them

---

*"Third countries" are those that are not party to a specific agreement.

wish to trade and that some have entered into agreements with the EEC, thus establishing the Association as a new dimension in international trade.

The first chapter is devoted to theoretical aspects of economic integration in an attempt to assess the nature of Association, and Chapter 2 describes the evolution of the system in some detail. The next three chapters explore the impact of Associaton on Africa: the Association-Commonwealth convergence (Chapter 3), trade between associates and the European Community (Chapter 4), and the special case of South Africa (Chapter 5). The rest of the book is concerned with worldwide ramifications of the Association System; discussion of GATT's views on trade preferences (Chapter 6) is followed by an outline of the development of Generalized Preferences and the part played by the Association in this respect (Chapter 7). Chapter 8 supports the view that GATT's principle of nondiscrimination has been a failure and Chapter 9 outlines sources of conflict in international trade. The conclusions are contained in Chapter 10.

MAP 1

The European Community and the Association System, 1976

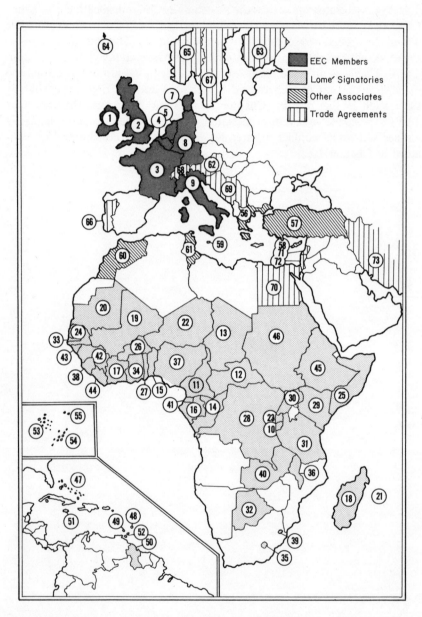

EEC Members

1 Ireland
2 Britian
3 France
4 Belgium
5 Netherlands

6 Luxembourg (not indicated)
7 Denmark
8 West Germany
9 Italy

Lomé Signatories

10 Burundi
11 Cameroon
12 Central African Republic
13 Chad
14 Congo
15 Benin
16 Gabon
17 Ivory Coast
18 Madagascar
19 Mali
20 Mauritania
21 Mauritius
22 Niger
23 Rwanda
24 Senegal
25 Somalia
26 Upper Volta
27 Togo
28 Zaïre
29 Kenya
30 Uganda
31 Tanzania
32 Botswana

33 Gambia
34 Ghana
35 Lesotho
36 Malawi
37 Nigeria
38 Sierra Leone
39 Swaziland
40 Zambia
41 Equatorial Guinea
42 Guinea
43 Guinea-Bissau
44 Liberia
45 Ethiopia
46 Sudan
47 Bahamas
48 Barbados
49 Grenada
50 Guyana
51 Jamaica
52 Trinidad & Tobago
53 Fiji
54 Tonga
55 Western Samoa

Other Associates

56 Greece
57 Turkey
58 Cyprus

59 Malta
60 Morocco
61 Tunisia

Trade Agreements

62 Austria
63 Finland
64 Iceland
65 Norway
66 Portugal
67 Sweden

68 Switzerland
69 Yugoslavia
70 Egypt
71 Lebanon
72 Israel
73 Iran

Association System of the European Community

ECONOMIC INTEGRATION

Economic integration is a recent development in international economics, both as a trade policy and as a field of study.

International trade policies vary with time and circumstances. The pendulum swung from the protectionism of the mercantilist period to the laissez-faire policies of the nineteenth century and back again to restrictionism at the beginning of the twentieth century due to the resurgence of nationalism. A severe depression and two world wars disrupted the world economy and efforts have been made in the last 30 years to return to freer trade.

Endeavors to restore stability in international economic relations took place on a global as well as on a regional scale. The United Nations, the International Monetary Fund, the Organization for European Economic Co-operation (OEEC), and the European Recovery Programme were all parts of this movement. More closely connected to international trade was the International Trade Organization (ITO)—which was never ratified—and the General Agreement on Tariffs and Trade (GATT), which has achieved a fair amount of success in trade liberalization since the first conference in Geneva in 1947.

On a regional scale, the growing realization that integration might be beneficial led some countries to investigate the possibility of some form of regional integration. There were two motives: politically, it was felt that closer links would increase the strength of their position among nations, and economically, integration was sought because it increases prospects of growth by widening the market and improving the scope for economies of scale and specialization.

Although customs unions existed before the last world war,* the practicability of establishing such unions was considered doubtful by economists of a protectionist era:

---

*The German Zollverein (1834), the South African Customs Union (1910), and the Economic Union between Belgium and Luxembourg (1921).

> When one reflects how difficult it often is, even in a unified state, to fix upon
> a tariff, owing to the conflict of wishes and opposition of interests of the
> various parties concerned, and when one remembers what a painful process
> it was to get an agreement between the two halves of the old Austria-
> Hungary, despite the bonds of a common monarch and a common army, one
> is forced to the conclusion that, apart from exceptional cases, these problems
> are practically insoluble.[1]

It was only during the 1950s and 1960s that economic integration gathered significant momentum in international economics.

After World War II, efforts were made to liberalize trade and reduce
nationalism. The results of international cooperation, however, proved disap-
pointing. The ITO failed, and the evolution of the Council of Europe and the
OEEC foiled the hopes of those who sought greater unity in Europe. On the
other hand, arrangements between a smaller group of countries—Benelux—
were progressing favorably. In 1951, the Treaty of Paris was signed, establishing the European Coal and Steel Community (ECSC) between the Six. Soon
after this, the European Economic Community and then the European Free
Trade Association were formed in Western Europe, followed by the Council
for Mutual Economic Assistance (COMECON) in the eastern part of the
continent. The African and Latin American integration schemes took shape
in the following decade, as also the Association System of the EEC. As is
well known, integration in Western Europe took two distinct forms: the loose
arrangements of EFTA, establishing free trade in industrial goods only, and
the closer integration of the economic union of the Six. The two groups have
now been linked by a series of trade agreements. There are, therefore, different
degrees and forms of economic integration.

Economic integration combines divided national economies into a single
economy. The first stages involve the removal of discriminatory measures
between countries and the more advanced steps include the coordination of
various policies into common policies.[2] Some countries never proceed beyond
the first stage while others integrate more fully. The process may be illustrated
as follows:

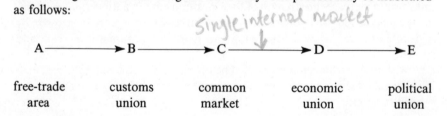

A ────────► B ──────── ► C ──────── ► D ──────── ► E
free-trade area	customs union	common market	economic union	political union

A *free-trade area* is the simplest form of economic integration. The
countries involved eliminate tariff barriers on the movement of goods between
themselves but they retain their own tariffs against goods from outside the

area. Examples of this type of integration are the European Free Trade Association and the Latin American Free Trade Area.

A *customs union* has two characteristics: the elimination of tariff barriers on the movement of goods—as in a free-trade area—and in addition a common external tariff on goods from outside the customs union. It establishes a common policy that requires agreement from the members of the union as to the type and extent of tariffs which will be applied. Thus it can be said that the customs union goes one step further than the free-trade area and that members of a customs union are more "integrated" than members of a free-trade area.

In a *common market,* there is free movement of all factors of production, involving not only goods, but also labor and capital. The EEC is often described as a common market although there still exist barriers to the movement of capital in the Community.

An *economic union* includes the characteristics of the common market but in addition there is coordination of national economic policies, which may necessitate harmonization of social, fiscal, and monetary policies. The EEC has harmonized policies in agriculture and external commercial relations and is currently establishing common policies in other sectors.

It may be controversial to place the *political union* at the end of the process, and some may prefer to consider this form of integration as total economic integration, but complete integration in all spheres of economic activity presupposes a supranational authority of such wide powers that it could only operate in a political union.

Although the above suggests integration as a gradual process from one form to another, this pattern is not always followed. The EEC proceeded straight away to a customs union without first establishing a free-trade area. In other words, the Six began to harmonize their common external tariff at the same time as eliminating tariff barriers between themselves. On the other hand, the Community has established common policies and can therefore be said to be an economic union, although—as mentioned above—restrictions on the movement of capital persist in some parts of the Community and therefore there is no common market in the exact sense of the term.

It may be asked where the monetary union should be placed in the integration process and one may be tempted to set it either before or after the economic union. However, the South African Customs Union is also a monetary union but as there are no plans to free the movement of labor, it is not a common market; the economic union between Belgium and Luxembourg has a common currency, but did not envisage a common agricultural policy until the EEC was established; the economic union of the EEC, on the other hand, may be a long way from achieving a common currency. In fact, the circumstances are such that a monetary union in Europe may well require some form of political union because of the far-reaching consequences of a common currency on all aspects of Community activities. The French economist Rueff has said, "L'Europe se fera par la monnaie."*

DEFINITION OF ECONOMIC INTEGRATION

From the point of view of terminology, there are differences of opinion as to the exact meaning of economic integration, and this has caused a certain ambiguity in discussions on the subject.

Balassa defines economic integration as a process and as a state of affairs.

> Regarded as a process, it encompasses measures designed to abolish discrimination between economic units belonging to different national states; viewed as a state of affairs, it can be represented by the absence of various forms of discrimination between national economies.[3]

Balassa further differentiates between economic union and total economic integration, where the former combines suppression of restrictions on factor movements and some degree of harmonization of national policies, while the latter is the unification of policies and requires a supranational authority whose decisions bind member states. This implies that other forms of integration do not need supranationalism, but even a customs union may decide to set up a council to decide on customs matters, and to give it supranational powers.

John Pinder adopts the narrower definition of economic integration as being the process of reaching the state of union, and "economic union as a state in which discrimination has been largely removed, and co-ordinated and common policies have been and are being applied on a sufficient scale."[4]

Pinder's terminology appears to clarify the problem but it does not help define the state of affairs that exists when countries begin the process of economic integration. Thus we must go back to Balassa's definition of economic integration as a process and a state of affairs and apply this formula to free trade areas, economic unions and other types of integration. There are two elements in integration: the process, which begins with a declaration of intention by the countries concerned; and the state of affairs, which is the result of measures taken to carry out these intentions. The Stockholm Convention of 1960 established the European Free Trade Association by announcing the intention of the "Seven" to establish a free-trade area, although the tariff barriers were not eliminated until several years later. The Benelux countries were regarded as an economic union long before the final treaty of 1958, which

---

*"Europe will be united through currency."

put the finishing touches on various measures taken by Belgium, the Netherlands, and Luxembourg from 1944 onward.

The intention of the signatories of the Treaty of Rome of 1957 was undoubtedly to form an economic union, even though a full customs union was not achieved until July 1968 and it will be many years before there is complete economic integration between the members. Moreover, there may always be some sector of the economy that evades the application of common policies.

Economic integration differs from economic cooperation in several respects. Economic cooperation such as is carried out under the auspices of the General Agreement on Tariffs and Trade aims at reducing discrimination and barriers to trade between countries by encouraging nondiscriminatory policies and the lowering of tariffs. With economic integration, there is to be complete suppression of discriminatory rules as well as the formation and application of common policies in a much wider area of economic activities. Another difference between cooperation and integration, and one that gives rise to conflict in international relations, is that cooperation tends to take place on a global scale whereas integration is only practicable on a regional scale. Economic integration is often referred to as "regional integration" to emphasize this aspect.

Economic integration implies the removal of barriers within a group of countries. This is a move toward free trade. At the same time, as it is only within the group that restrictive measures are abolished, those outside the area feel discriminated against and look upon the integration process as preferential arrangements from which they are excluded. Thus integration is a combination of free trade and discrimination. It is sometimes said that economic integration is a movement toward both free trade and protection, but this is not entirely correct. Protection depends on the height of the common external tariff: if this is lower than the tariffs of some of the members before integration, it cannot be said that there has been a move toward protection. It is therefore more accurate to say that economic integration is a movement toward free trade and discrimination. It is this dual aspect that has given rise to differences of attitudes toward integration and to the complexity of customs-union theory.

THEORIES OF ECONOMIC INTEGRATION

The theory of economic integration can be regarded as a part of international economics, but it also enlarges the field of international trade theory by exploring the impact of a fusion of national markets on growth and examining the need for the coordination of economic policies in a union.[5]

Theoretical analyses of economic integration began in about 1950 with the works of Jacob Viner, Maurice Byé, and Herbert Giersch, although the most often quoted today is Viner's theory of customs unions.[6] Before this, a customs union was assumed to be difficult to achieve but generally beneficial since it increased the area of free trade. However, Viner pointed out that this was not always so. Two changes are likely to occur after the formation of a customs union, namely trade-diversion and trade-creation, and the overall effect will be favorable only if there is more trade-creation than trade-diversion.

Consider three countries A, B, and C and goods X and Y. Good X is produced at low cost in C and at high cost in B, while good Y is produced at low cost in B and at high cost in A. Country A applies nondiscriminatory tariffs on all imports. Prior to the formation of the customs union, A imports good X from C and buys good Y from local producers because, although good Y is produced at lower cost in B, the tariff is such that it would be more expensive to import Y from B.

Countries A and B enter into a customs union and abolish tariffs between them, but maintain tariffs on imports from C. Given a certain common external tariff and ignoring transport costs, A will then buy good X from B because it is cheaper than the cost of X from C plus tariff. This is trade-diversion and is held to be harmful because it diverts trade from low-cost to high-cost producers. On the other hand, A will now also buy good Y from B, because B is a low-cost producer of Y and tariffs no longer protect the high-cost producers in A. This is called trade-creation by Viner, but it is in fact trade-diversion of another kind. Trade has not increased as such, but interregional trade has been replaced by international trade. The beneficial effect is due to the fact that A is now buying from low-cost producers instead of from local high-cost producers.

The mechanism is more doubtful in the case of a free-trade area, since each country is free to decide on its own tariffs, and differences in the heights of tariffs for the same good distort the picture, before and after the formation of the free-trade area. In a theory of free-trade area, H. Shibata compares customs unions and free-trade areas, but he does not conclude that one type is better than another, since the effects of both

> depend on a large number of unknown parameters and variables involved in a large number of demand and supply schedules of the commodities thus affected.[7]

Customs-union theory was refined and expanded, notably by J. E. Meade, R. G. Lipsey, and H. G. Johnson, but it fails to prove that customs unions are either beneficial or harmful to members of the union or to the world as a whole. Consequently, new fields of research have been explored.

Quantitative estimates have been carried out to assess the likely gains from free trade in Western Europe, notably the calculations of Verdoorn and of Johnson.

The result, when compared to annual national incomes, showed gains from
freer trade to be exceedingly small; Verdoorn's calculations yielded a figure
of 0.05 per cent of national income, while Johnson arrived at a *maximum*
figure of 1.0 per cent of national income.[8]

These low results have been regarded as insignificant since it is now
generally accepted that the static gains of a customs union are less important
than the dynamic effects of the union, such as effects on growth, competition,
and investments. It is also admitted that economic integration often takes place
for political rather than economic reasons, and it is felt that "economic analysis would be more fruitfully focused on the implications for economic policy
of the existence of customs unions than on the justification of customs unions
in terms of forecast changes in the flows of trade."[9]

In recent years, economists have turned their attention to the special
problems of developing countries. Their usual trade pattern of exporting primary products and importing manufactured goods has not contributed greatly
to their development. They are caught in a dilemma. To achieve greater
stability of primary goods prices and an improvement in terms of trade,
developing countries need economic development and the ability to reallocate
resources, but in order to improve economic development, they need stable and
higher prices to earn more foreign exchange.

In their efforts to improve their position, some developing countries are
attempting to form customs unions and free-trade areas, in spite of the fact that
opinions are divided on the benefits they are likely to reap from economic
integration.[10]

The problem centers on the competitiveness or complementarity of the
two economies. Thus if the customs union is taking place between a developed
and developing economy, the advanced region will always be ahead in production and technology. Capital will flow to the dynamic area, where the infrastructure will improve comparatively more than in the weaker area, and higher
wages will attract the best labor from the developing economy, thus depressing
it further. This argument may or may not be correct. But the important thing
is to realize that, at the present state of the theory and of the evidence on this
subject, it is impossible to *know* whether, or in what circumstances, the argument is correct or not.[11]

Whatever the findings of economists, several developing countries have
begun the process of economic integration. Some have formed customs unions
and free-trade areas with each other (for example, East African Economic
Community, Central African Customs and Economic Union, Latin American
Free Trade Area, Central American Common Market) and others have entered into free-trade areas with the European Economic Community.

The question of world welfare has sometimes been raised: do customs
unions increase or decrease total welfare? There is no clear-cut answer and the

point is rather theoretical since countries enter into customs unions in the hope of increasing their own welfare and not that of the whole world.

It is beyond the scope of this book to delve further into new developments of integration theory. It must be admitted that there is no consensus of opinion in customs union theory except as regards its complexity. It is of interest to note, however, that J. E. Meade, after spending a great deal of time and effort on the theory of trade-creation and trade-diversion, wrote that if he were a citizen of a Benelux country he would support it strongly even if a careful estimate suggested that it was more likely to reduce rather than to raise economic welfare in the narrow sense of the term, because "larger social and political units are likely to be more viable and self-reliant politically and strategically [and] there is a need for greater integration of the countries of the free world."[12]

This brief outline of economic integration should help to place the Association System of the EEC into a relevant framework and to understand the nature of the agreements that established this particular form of integration. However, in common with the point made by John Pinder, this book is focused on the implications of the existence of the Association System and is not concerned with a justification or condemnation of this aspect of the EEC's external relations.

NOTES

1. Gottfried von Haberler, *The Theory of International Trade with Its Application to Commercial Policy* (London: W. Hodge, 1933 [English translation, 1950]), p. 391.

2. These have been called "negative" and "positive" integration by Jan Tinbergen, *International Economic Integration* (Amsterdam: Elsevier, 1954), p. 122.

3. Bela Balassa, *The Theory of Economic Integration* (Homewood, Ill.: Richard D. Irwin, 1961), p. 1.

4. John Pinder, "Problems of European Integration," in *Economic Integration in Europe,* ed. G. R. Denton (London: Weidenfeld and Nicolson, 1969), p. 145.

5. Balassa, *The Theory of Economic Integration,* p. 3.

6. Jacob Viner, *The Customs Union Issue* (New York: Carnegie Endowment for International Peace, 1950). Maurice Byé, "Unions Douanières et Données Nationales," *Economie Appliquée* (January/March 1950): 121–58. (The English translation was published in *International Economic Papers,* no. 3 [London: Macmillan, 1953], pp. 208–34). Herbert Giersch, "Economic Union between Nations and the Location of Industries," *Review of Economic Studies* 17 (2), no. 43 (1949–50): 87–97.

7. H. Shibata, "A Theory of Free Trade Areas," in *International Economic Integration,* ed. Peter Robson (Harmondsworth: Penguin, 1972), p. 83. Reprinted from C. Shoup, ed., *Fiscal Harmonization in Common Markets* (New York: Columbia University Press, 1967), vol. 1, sections 4 and 5.

8. H. H. Liesner, "Regional Free Trade: Trade-Creating and Trade-Diverting Effects of Political, Commercial and Monetary Areas," in *International Trade in a Developing World,* eds. Roy Harrod and D. C. Hague (London: Macmillan, 1963), p. 198.

9. Pinder, "Problems of European Integration," p. 148.

10. See F. Kahnert, et al., *Economic Integration among Developing Countries* (Paris: Development Centre of the Organization for Economic Cooperation and Development, 1969). See R. F. Mikesell, "The Theory of Common Markets as Applied to Regional Arrangements among Developing Countries," in *International Trade in a Developing World,* eds. Harrod and Hague, pp. 205–29.

11. Pinder, "Problems of European Integration," p. 153.

12. J. E. Meade, *The Theory of Customs Unions* (Amsterdam: North-Holland, 1955), pp. 114–15.

2

THE ASSOCIATION SYSTEM OF
THE EUROPEAN ECONOMIC
COMMUNITY

The Association System of the European Economic Community was established in 1957 to govern relations between the Six and their dependencies in the field of trade and cooperation. The legal basis for this relationship can be found in Article 131 of the Treaty of Rome, which reads: "The purpose of this Association shall be to promote the economic and social development of the countries and territories and to establish close economic relations between them and the Community as a whole." (See Appendix A for relevant articles of the Treaty of Rome, 1957.) Since then, the Association has altered in nature, size, and complexity. (See Table 1.)

As this book is concerned with the impact of the Association on international trade policies, the nature and evolution of this system must first be outlined. The purpose of this chapter is therefore to explain the Association System and the different types of agreements involved, and to examine the reaction of nonmembers and the various criticisms that have been aimed at the Association since its inception.

It is important, at the outset, to differentiate between three types of agreements that are in force at the moment:

The most important agreement is the Lomé Convention, signed in 1975 in the capital of Togo, West Africa, between 9 European Community members and 46 African, Caribbean, and Pacific states (ACP). This agreement replaces the Yaounde Conventions of 1963 and 1969—which established the Association of African and Malagasy States (AAMS). The Yaounde Associates totaled 18 until Mauritius joined them in 1972. Although the terms vary slightly, both Lomé and Yaounde Conventions established what may be regarded as "full" Association.

A special type of Association was created under Article 238 of the Rome Treaty: "The Community may conclude with a third country, a union of States

TABLE 1
The Association System as of January 1, 1976

FULL ASSOCIATION ⟹ *Articles 131-6*

1. Under Part IV of the Treaty of
   Rome, 1957[a]

2. Yaounde Convention I and	Burundi	Gabon	Rwanda
	Cameroon	Ivory Coast	Senegal
3. Yaounde Convention II, 1963 and 1969	Central African Republic	Malagasy	Somalia
		Mali	Togo
	Chad	Mauritania	Upper Volta
	Congo	Mauritius[b]	Zaïre
	Dahomey	Niger	

4. Lomé Convention, 1975
   Yaounde associates, plus:
   Commonwealth

Africa	Botswana	Lesotho	Swaziland
	Gambia	Malawi	Tanzania
	Ghana	Nigeria	Uganda
	Kenya	Sierra Leone	Zambia
Caribbean	Bahamas	Grenada	Jamaica
	Barbados	Guyana	Trinidad & Tobago
Pacific	Fiji	Tonga	Western Somoa
Others			
Africa	Equatorial Guinea	Ethiopia	Guinea–Bissau
	Sudan	Guinea	Liberia

SPECIAL ASSOCIATION → *Article 238*

1. Aiming at full membership	Greece, 1961	Turkey, 1963
2. Others	Morocco, 1969	Malta, 1971
	Tunisia, 1969	Cyprus, 1972

TRADE AGREEMENTS → *Article 113*

1. Mediterranean area	Lebanon, 1964	Yugoslavia, 1970
	Israel, 1964	Egypt, 1972
	Spain, 1970	
2. EFTA countries, 1972–73	Austria	Portugal
	Finland	Sweden
	Iceland	Switzerland
	Norway	
3. Others	Iran, 1963	Sri Lanka, 1972
	Pakistan, 1968	Brazil, 1973
	Argentina, 1971	India, 1973
	Indonesia, 1972	Uruguay, 1973
	Thailand, 1972	Bangladesh, 1973
	Philippines, 1972	

[a] See Appendix B.
[b] Joined in 1972.
Note: Dates indicate initial participation.
Source: Compiled by the author.

11

or an international organisation, agreements creating an association embodying reciprocal rights and obligations, joint actions and special procedures."
These agreements are sui generis, some of them leading up to future membership, as in the case of Greece and Turkey, while others only envisage a limited
Association, as was the case for the East African territories under the Arusha
agreement of 1969. This is sometimes called "special" or "partial" Association.

Lastly, the EEC has entered into purely commercial agreements with
certain countries, mostly in the Mediterranean area, but also recently with
members of the European Free Trade Association, which did not join the
Common Market. It is not always easy to distinguish between special association agreements and trade agreements. Some writers may prefer to omit trade
agreements from a review of the Association System, but they are included
here because, in spite of the fact that countries that enter into trade agreements
with the EEC are not associates, the links they form with the Community are
of a similar nature to those formed by special association agreements. A list
of association and trade agreements as of January 1, 1976 is included in Table
1.

FULL ASSOCIATION

Full Association is the most comprehensive type of association, but without the prospect of eventual membership of the European Community, because
according to Article 237 of the Treaty of Rome, only European countries may
join the Community.

The number of countries involved in 1957 decreased slightly when the first
arrangement was replaced by the Yaounde Convention of 1963, but doubled
with the Lomé Convention of 1975. Thus the Association progressed through
four stages: Association under the Treaty of Rome, 1957–63; Association of
African and Malagasy States created by the Yaounde Convention, 1963–69;
Second Yaounde Convention, 1969–75; and the Lomé Convention, since 1975.
An examination of each stage will explain the nature of the relationship
between the EEC and associates.

Association under the Treaty of Rome, 1957

The basis of this association is outlined in Part IV of the Rome Treaty,
Articles 131 to 136.* The purpose of the Association is to promote the social

---

*See Appendix A.

and economic development of those territories that were dependencies of EEC members, and to establish close economic relationship between those countries and the Community. The Association System contains two main elements, namely, rules regulating trade between the EEC and associates, and financial aid. The territories concerned were listed in Annex IV of the Treaty of Rome. They included French and Dutch dependencies, the Belgian Congo, the Trusteeship of Ruanda-Urundi, and Italian Somaliland.*

The background to the inclusion of Articles 131–36 in the Treaty of Rome was as follows. When the Six decided to form the EEC, those members who still had dependencies asked that a solution be found to avoid breaking the links between the metropolitan countries and those dependencies, a severance that could have had detrimental effects on both sides. France suggested extending the economic union to colonies but this was rejected, especially by Germany. It must be remembered that Germany had lost her colonies at the end of World War I and this may have influenced her views. France, however, took the position that she would not join the EEC unless some arrangement was made with regard to those territories. Although France was the most interested party, due to the size of her colonial empire, one must not underestimate the interest of Belgium and Italy in the matter. After a great deal of discussion and negotiations, which at times threatened the creation of the EEC, the Association arrangements were accepted by all members.

The main features of the 1957 Association were:

Financial aid to the associates, through the establishment of a European Development Fund.

Gradual abolition of tariffs between the EEC and the associates, and between the associates themselves, except where international obligations prevented this, but with authorization to levy customs duties in certain circumstances, such as for the protection of infant industries.

Absence of discrimination between members of the EEC with regard to the application of these duties.

Freedom of movement for workers between the associated territories and the EEC.

Right of establishment of nationals and companies of EEC members in those territories.

There were a few exceptions to the preferential system thus established. For instance, Germany was allowed a duty-free quota for the import of bananas from nonassociates, while Italy and the Benelux countries were granted a similar quota on unroasted coffee.

---

*See Appendix B for list of territories associated under Part IV of the Treaty of Rome, 1957.

The 1957 Association set up a free-trade area between the Six and their dependencies. A customs union already existed between France and her colonies, but not between Belgium and the Congo, because the Congo Basin Treaties of 1885 and 1890 precluded discrimination in customs matters.[1] The main change introduced by the Rome Treaty, Part IV, was the extension of this Common Market to other members of the EEC. From 1957 onward, all members of the Community began to abolish tariffs on goods from those territories, thus giving exports from associates preferential treatment over exports from nonassociates.

The Association System set up by the EEC was criticized from the start by a number of third countries. "The creation of this preferential system evoked loud protests in the GATT from Latin American and other African countries such as Ghana who claimed that this preference would seriously harm their exports to the member states."[2] This particular aspect will be examined later. It must be stressed here, however, that the preferential regime between France and her overseas territories, and between the Benelux countries and their dependencies, was allowed under the GATT. Article 1(2) of the General Agreement specifically allows long-standing preferences. It is only the extension of these preferential arrangements to other members of the EEC which was vulnerable under the GATT rules.

First Yaounde Convention, 1963

Soon after 1960, most of the African territories associated with the Common Market gained independence. Since new African states could not be bound by the Treaty of Rome, which had been signed only by the Six, a new arrangement was required. The issue was complicated by the prospect of British entry into the EEC, because Britain wanted to establish a link between the Community and Commonwealth countries, possibly an extension of the Association, at least to African countries. Moreover, differences of opinion were apparent between members of the EEC as to the form of the prospective Association. By January 1963, however, without waiting for the result of the British negotiations, an agreement was reached between the Six and 18 of the 1957 associates, and a Convention was signed at Yaounde, Cameroon, in July 1963, establishing the Association of African and Malagasy States (AAMS).* The Eighteen were: Burundi, Cameroon, Central African Republic, Chad, Congo, Zaïre, Dahomey, Gabon, Ivory Coast, Malagasy Republic,

---

*See Appendix C.

Mali, Mauritania, Niger, Rwanda, Senegal, Somalia,* Togo and Upper Volta. Guinea refused to join the AAMS.

Part IV of the Treaty of Rome remained effective and deals with relations between the EEC and the remaining dependencies of France and the Netherlands: New Caledonia, French Polynesia, Wallis and Futuna, the Comores Islands, French Territory of the Afars and Issas, Saint Pierre and Miquelon, the French Southern and Antarctic territories, Surinam and Netherlands Antilles. The Association between the EEC and Netherlands New Guinea ended in 1963, when this country became part of Indonesia. The 1957 Association does not apply to the French overseas departments of Guiana, Martinique, Guadeloupe, and Réunion.

Although the Yaounde Association had the same broad purpose as the earlier arrangement, namely trade expansion, financial aid, and the right of establishment, there were several differences between the two systems.

Whereas the 1957 Association was signed by the Six on behalf of their dependencies, the Yaounde Convention was agreed upon by the Common Market countries and 18 associates. Thus, the earlier system was an arrangement by metropolitan countries dealing with their colonies, while the 1963 Convention was freely agreed upon by newly independent African states. The point has sometimes been raised as to whether those developing countries were in fact free to adhere to the Association established at Yaounde, since they were economically dependent on the continuation of this arrangement. But although the Eighteen may have needed special links with the EEC, they were at liberty, legally and constitutionally, to sign the Convention or remain out of the new scheme, as illustrated by the fact that Guinea, once a French colony, decided to withdraw from the group of the 1957 associates, and has remained outside the Association until 1975, when she became a signatory to the Lomé Convention.

The Treaty of Rome, Part IV, provided for the abolition of customs duties between the Six and the Eighteen, and also between the associates, thus establishing one large free-trade area. The Yaounde Convention, on the other hand, established 18 free-trade areas, between the EEC and each of the 18 associates.† The reason for this is that interassociate trade is outside the scope of the Convention. The associates are free to organize their trade with each other, and with third countries, as each of them thinks fit. Article 8 of the Convention

---

*Somalia includes Italian and British Somaliland; French Somaliland is now the French territory of the Afars and Issas.

†There were a few exceptions. Agricultural products competing with the EEC products receive preferential treatment instead of free entry into the Community. Due to international obligations, Zaïre and Togo do not give preferences to EEC products.

of Association states that, "this Convention shall not preclude the maintenance or establishment of customs unions or free-trade areas among Associated States"; and Article 9 reads, "this Convention shall not preclude the
maintenance or establishment of customs unions or free-trade areas between
one or more Associated States and one or more third countries insofar as they
neither are nor prove to be incompatible with the principles and provisions of
the said Convention." So far, five associates have formed an economic union:
l'Union Douaniére et Economique de l'Afrique Centrale (UDEAC),* created
in 1964 between the Congo, Gabon, Central African Republic, Chad, and
Cameroon, but none have attempted integration with nonassociates.

The fact that the Yaounde Convention of 1963 established 18 free-
trade areas instead of one, as in the case of the earlier Association, is considered
by some writers as a backward step. In the sense that the large free-trade area
has broken up into 18 free-trade areas, it is further away from the ideal of trade
liberalization. On the other hand, the 1957 Association was decided upon by
six countries—the EEC—whereas the Yaounde Convention was signed by 24
nations and therefore should be accepted as a step forward in international
economic cooperation.

Whereas the EEC institutions administered the 1957 Association, Article
39 of the Yaounde Convention provided for an Association Council assisted
by an Association Committee, a Parliamentary Conference and a Court of
Arbitration. The salient features of these institutions were as follows: The
Association Council was composed "on the one hand, of the members of the
Council of the EEC and members of the Commission of the EEC, and on the
other hand, of one member of the Government of each Associated State"
(Article 40).

> The Association Council shall express itself by mutual agreement between
> the Community on the one hand and the Associated States on the other. The
> Community ... and the Associated States ... shall each by means of an
> internal Protocol determine their procedure for arriving at their respective
> positions (Article 43).

This means that each side had only one vote, and that all decisions had to be
reached by unanimity. The main functions of the Council were consultation,
deliberation, and supervision over the implementation of the Convention. It
was assisted by an Association Committee, which assumed considerable significance since the Council only met once a year.[3]

The Parliamentary Conference consisted of an equal number of delegates
from the European Assembly and from the parliaments of the associated

---

*Central African Customs and Economic Union.

states, but as in the case of the European Assembly, its powers were very limited. It met once a year.

The Court of Arbitration judged disputes concerning the interpretation and application of the Convention and could make binding decisions if prior amicable settlement by the Council had failed. It was composed of five members: a president, appointed by the Council, and "four judges chosen from among persons whose independence and competence can be fully guaranteed" (Articles 51 and 52).

Apart from the above changes, the Yaounde Convention differed from the 1957 Association on a few other minor points. On the other hand, escape clauses were retained such as in Article 13, which allowed one or more associated states to take measures such as tariffs and quantitative restrictions, "if serious disturbances occur in one sector of the economy or jeopardize its external financial stability," and in Article 3 which permitted associates to retain or even introduce customs duties which "correspond to their development needs or their industrialization requirements or which are intended to contribute to their budget."

Second Yaounde Convention, 1969

Some doubts were expressed in various quarters as to whether the Yaounde Convention would be renewed after its expiration in 1969. Besides differences of opinion between EEC members as to the content of the future Convention, especially between France and Germany, there was evidence of pressure on the EEC, from nonassociated countries, mainly Latin America, not to renew the Convention. The Group of 77 of the United Nations Conference for Trade and Development (UNCTAD) was actively trying to establish the Generalized Scheme of Preferences (GSP) whereby developed countries would give preferential treatment to manufactured goods from developing nations, and this was felt by some to be an alternative to the Association preferential system.* However, the associates pressed for the renewal of the Convention, and this was carried out at Yaounde in July 1969.

In terms of this Convention, certain provisions on financial aid were altered, the Six increasing the European Development Fund's resources from $730 million for the 1964–69 period, to $918 million for the next five years. However, the African associates had hoped for a bigger increase and expressed dissatisfaction. In order to reduce the discriminatory effects of the agreement on the trade of nonassociates, the common external tariff of the EEC was

---

*See Chapter 7. The Group of 77 is made up of active developing countries within the framework of UNCTAD and actually comprises 112 countries.

lowered for some products, for example, coffee, cocoa beans, and palm oil. This reduction in the margin of preferences upset the associates, but it was a compromise between the conflicting demands of the two groups: the associates wanting to perpetuate preferential treatment, and third countries wishing to minimize it.

Extension of the Yaounde Association to Mauritius

Article 58 of the Yaounde Convention provided for accession to the Association, of "States which have an economic structure and production comparable to those Associated States." Mauritius was the first country to have become associated under this provision. By an agreement signed in May 1972, the EEC granted Mauritius duty-free access for most of her exports to the Community, as far as industrial goods are concerned. Farm produce received preferential treatment but sugar was temporarily excepted, because Mauritius sugar benefited from a guaranteed outlet to the United Kingdom under the Commonwealth Sugar Agreement. On the other hand, EEC goods were to receive the same treatment as Commonwealth goods imported into Mauritius.

The important aspect of this agreement, which brought the number of Yaounde associates to 19, was that Mauritius was the first Commonwealth country to become a full associate of the EEC. Previously, Commonwealth States had entered into either special association agreements or trade agreements. The only exception was ex-British Somaliland, which became associated in 1963, but only because it joined ex-Italian Somaliland to form Somalia in 1960.

Lomé Convention, 1975

British entry into the EEC made it necessary to reconsider the relationship between the Community and Africa, since it would affect trade links between Britain and Commonwealth countries. During the negotiations leading to the Treaty of Accession of January 1972, whereby Britain, Ireland, and Denmark joined the European Community, it was decided to offer developing Commonwealth countries, as well as nations with an economic structure similar to that of Yaounde associates, some form of formal relationship with the Community. Those countries, most of which were in Africa, were given three choices: full Association on the lines of the Yaounde Convention, a more limited Association, such as that already linking Kenya, Tanzania, and Uganda to the EEC (see the Arusha Convention, discussed on page 27), or a simple trade agreement.

At the same time, the expiry of Yaounde II in 1975 necessitated a reappraisal of the arrangements between the EEC and Yaounde associates. It was considered appropriate to combine the two, and for the enlarged Community to negotiate with both the Commonwealth group and Yaounde associates. A few other countries such as Ethiopia and the Sudan were also interested.

Negotiations took about three years. At the beginning, some Commonwealth countries showed distrust of the concept of Association with which they were not well acquainted. Nigeria, in particular, feared that Association with the EEC would lead to a subordinate status for developing states. This was paradoxical, since Nigeria had been the first Commonwealth country to enter into an association agreement with the EEC (see the discussion of the Lagos Convention on page 27).

Among problems discussed during negotiations was that of "reverse preferences," the stipulation that trade concessions should be reciprocal. This was a basic GATT principle and some EEC members felt it should be maintained. On the other hand, most of the English-speaking African countries regarded this reciprocity as no longer justified and quoted the newly established Generalized System of Preferences (see Chapter 7) as a case in point. It was stressed that the GATT waives the rule of reciprocity where developing countries are concerned. In the end, the EEC agreed to abandon reverse preferences but asked for a guarantee of most-favored-nation treatment and nondiscrimination between EEC members.

Formally opened in July 1973, negotiations continued through a conference in Brussels in October, then at Addis Ababa, Ethiopia, in February 1974, and at Kingston, Jamaica, the following July. Since the Yaounde Convention was to end on January 31, 1975, a sense of urgency began to be felt by the negotiators. Discussions were resumed later in 1974, but a final agreement was only reached on the morning of February 1, 1975, when 9 EEC and 46 African, Caribbean, and Pacific (ACP) countries signed the Lomé Convention (see Appendix D for full text of agreement) in the Togo capital.

One of the most interesting aspects of these negotiations was the cohesion of the ACP countries. Despite the difficulties of coordinating so many different viewpoints, Francophone and Anglophone negotiators showed a remarkably united front in their dealings with EEC spokesmen. This African unity in economic affairs contrasts with the division in the Organization for African Unity (OAU) vote on Angola in January 1976, when 22 states voted for the (MPLA) Movimento Popular Libertaçao de Angola* and 22 against, each side comprising a substantial number of Commonwealth and Yaounde nations.

---

*Popular Movement for Liberation of Angola.

The Lomé Convention provides for the accession of any state with an economic structure comparable to that of ACP states, as long as the original signatories give their consent. Thus the door is open for Angola and Mozambique to join the Lomé associates if they wish.

The Lomé Convention is divided into six parts: trade cooperation; export earnings from commodities; industrial cooperation; financial and technical cooperation; establishment, services, payments, and capital movements; and institutions. In addition, the agreement includes several protocols with specific topics such as sugar, rum, and bananas.

Trade Cooperation

The EEC is giving free access to most exports from ACP countries and in return, these will give EEC products most-favored-nation treatment and they will not discriminate between Community members. Access to the Community's markets will be free where customs duties are the only form of protection. It has been estimated that 94.2 percent of ACP agricultural exports will enter duty-free.[4] For 5.8 percent, however, there remain restrictions due to the Common Agricultural Policy of the EEC, but those ACP exports will nevertheless receive preferential treatment. This affects products that compete with EEC agricultural goods, such as beef, veal, certain fruit, and vegetables.

Although these restrictions apply only to a small percentage of ACP products as a whole, for specific countries it concerns a much larger part of their trade. In the case of Botswana, for instance, livestock amounts to about 80 percent of their exports. As this could nullify the advantages of the Lomé Convention for some countries, the ministers of foreign affairs of the Community agreed on June 26, 1975, to suspend 90 percent of the import levy on beef imports from Botswana, Swaziland, Kenya, and Madagascar. This was a temporary measure and it was hoped that the ACP would start exporting a different cut of beef that would not compete with EEC goods and would therefore not be subject to the import levy.

Export Earnings

This section institutes a new method of stabilizing export earnings of ACP countries. The system is called STABEX and is applicable to 12 basic products.* It works as follows: Where an ACP country's earnings from the export of one of the specified products represents at least 7.5 percent (2.5 percent for

---

*See Appendix D, Article 17 for list of products concerned.

the 34 least-developed, land-locked, or island ACP) of its total export earnings, that state is entitled to a financial transfer if its annual earnings from the export of that product to the EEC fall to 7.5 percent (2.5 percent for the least-developed, land-locked, or island ACP) below the "reference level." This level is calculated on the basis of the average of the four previous years. In the case of Burundi, Ethiopia, Guinea-Bissau, Rwanda, and Swaziland, the system will apply to exports of the products listed, irrespective of destination.

The Community will provide 375 million unit-of-account* (MUA) to the STABEX fund, but provision is also made for a certain amount of self-help because the ACP states that have received transfers are to contribute to the reconstitution of resources, when certain conditions have been met, five years after receipt of aid. Twenty-four countries are exempt from this obligation.

Industrial Cooperation

The Community will help to set up programs and projects as regards infrastructures, industrial undertakings, training, technology, and research, in order to promote the industrial development of the ACP states. A Committee on Industrial Cooperation will gather and disseminate information, and organize and facilitate contacts between commercial agents.

Financial and Technical Cooperation

The Community will contribute toward the European Development Fund (originally created under the Rome Treaty of 1957) for the economic and social development of associates. The fund will provide grants and loans to the ACP, and certain measures were taken to guarantee the optimum use of those funds; for example, the EEC Commission will be represented in each state by a delegate responsible for the correct implementation of projects financed from the fund. At present, the fund consists of 3,000 MAU† distributed as follows:

> 2,100 grants
> 430 soft loans (1 percent interest)
> 95 risk capital
> 375 STABEX

---

*The EEC unit-of-account is made up of specified amounts of the member currencies. In March 1975, its value was approximately $1.31.

†Commission of the European Communities, Information: Development and Cooperation, *The Signing of the Lomé Convention*, 88/75, p. 8.

In addition, the European Investment Bank will contribute 390 MUA in the form of normal loans.

Establishment, Services, Payments, and Capital Movements

The purpose of these measures is to provide nondiscriminatory treatment of EEC nationals or companies in ACP states and similarly, equal treatment of ACP nationals and companies in the Community. The signatories should also refrain from using any measures that would render impossible the fulfillment of obligations undertaken under the Convention.

Institutions

Three bodies are set up: the Council of Ministers, assisted by the Committee of Ambassadors, and the Consultative Assembly. They are run on similar lines to those of the Yaounde Association.

The Council of Ministers is composed of EEC Council members and EEC Commission members on the one hand, and a government member of each ACP state on the other hand. This Council will meet once a year and whenever the necessity arises. It may delegate certain powers to the Committee of Ambassadors, which is the body generally responsible for assisting it in the performance of its duties.

The Consultative Assembly is made up, on a joint and equal basis, of members of the European Assembly representing the Community and of representatives appointed by the ACP states. It expresses its opinions in the form of resolutions on matters covered by the Convention. There is also an arbitration procedure for settling disputes regarding the interpretation or implementation of the agreement.

Protocols

Among the protocols attached to the Convention, the most important is the one dealing with trade in sugar. For an indefinite period, the Community undertakes to buy up to 1,375,000 metric tons of sugar from the ACP at guaranteed prices. These prices will be fixed each year and will be within the range of prices operating for sugar produced within the EEC. The sugar will be first offered on the market and the Community will purchase only if the guaranteed price cannot be reached on the free market.

The Lomé Convention will expire in 1980.

Comparing the Lomé and Yaounde Conventions, it can be said that, on the whole, the latest agreement improves the position of associates vis-a-vis the

European Community. As usual in an agreement of this kind, however, the ACP countries wanted more than the EEC was prepared to grant.

The most important change is obviously the extension of Association to all independent African States and—although marginally—to other continents, Caribbean and Pacific territories. This was achieved in spite of persistent criticism of the Association System, mainly in English-speaking areas. Not one Commonwealth African state rejected the offer and Guinea, an ex-French territory that had kept aloof from the Yaounde Association, now also joined the ACP countries.

The main differences between the two Conventions concern trade arrangements, STABEX, and financial cooperation. The Lomé Convention does not create free-trade areas as the Yaounde Convention did, but this was in answer to a variety of pressures on the EEC to give up "reverse preferences." For example, the United States had made the extension of its Generalized System of Preferences to EEC associates, dependent on the abolition of reverse preferences. The ACP countries will now qualify for the benefits of the U.S. GSP, recently implemented.

It has been said that now ACP countries may give preferential treatment to other developing countries, but this was also the case under the Yaounde Convention, since Articles 8 and 9 allowed associates to form customs unions or free-trade areas both with other associates or nonassociates. In any case, the Yaounde Convention established free-trade areas in which, by definition, members are free to impose the import tariff they wish on third countries.

The second innovation is the arrangement for stabilizing export earnings of ACP countries, and the third is the increase of funds available for aid. Although this has increased threefold, inflation and the fact that the population of the ACP is far larger than that of the AAMS (Nigeria alone has a population of 60 million) means that the amount available per capita is less than under the Yaounde Convention. This, however, is inevitable since the newcomers to the Community—Britain, Ireland, and Denmark—are not in a position to contribute large amounts to Community aid, and on the other hand, the population of associates as a whole has doubled. It should also be noted that these aid measures were taken at a time when most Western countries were experiencing an economic recession.

SPECIAL ASSOCIATION AGREEMENTS

In the last decade, the Community has entered into a variety of Association agreements with nonmember countries. The Treaty of Rome provides for these agreements in Article 238: "The EEC may conclude with a nonmember state, a union between states or an international organization, agreements creating an association characterised by reciprocal rights and obligations, communal actions and particular procedures."

The terms of these arrangements vary. Most of them establish preferential entry into the EEC, for exports from associates and the so-called "reverse preferences," that is, preferential entry into the associated countries for exports from the EEC. Several associates receive financial aid, others do not. Agreements are signed for a specific period, usually three to six years. They are renewable and revokable according to a procedure laid down in each agreement. A brief outline of the most important of these agreements will suffice to illustrate their diversity. "Special" associates are situated in two main areas: the Mediterranean region and Africa.

Mediterranean Region

Most countries bordering the Mediterranean have entered into agreements with the EEC, Albania, Syria, and Libya being exceptions to the rule. Algeria is negotiating. Some of these arrangements have established an association with the Community, while others have been simple trade agreements, which will be discussed later.

Among the association agreements sui generis, a distinction must be drawn between those entered into with a view of eventual membership of the EEC and those that do not envisage this possibility. Only the agreements with Greece and Turkey aim at full membership of the Community.

Greece and Turkey

As the Association agreements with these two countries are similar, they can be examined together. Greece became an associate in 1961, and Turkey in 1963. Article 2 of each agreement states that the long-range objective is

> to promote a continuous and balanced strengthening of the commercial and economic relations between the contracting parties with full consideration of the need to ensure the accelerated development of the economy of [Greece, Turkey] as well as the elevation of the level of employment and of the living standards of the [Greek, Turkish] people.

To achieve this, the intermediate objectives are a customs union between the EEC and each country, and the harmonization of economic policies, while the long-term aim is full membership.[5] The establishment of the customs union will not take place according to the same timetable since the states of the economies of Greece and Turkey differ.

In the agreement with Greece, it was decided that customs duties would be abolished over a 12-year period except for a few items that needed protection, in which case the period would extend to 22 years. Turkey, with a lower level of development, was to go through a "preparatory" period during the first five years, when the Community would give preferential tariff quotas to Turkish exports of tobacco, dried grapes, and a few other commodities representing about 40 percent of Turkey's exports to the EEC. This would be followed by the "transition" period, during which Turkey and the EEC would move toward a customs union. Turkey is now in the transition stage. The agreement with Greece, which suffered a setback with the 1967 coup d'etat, has now reached the stage of negotiation, and within a few years Greece should become the tenth member of the European Community.

The institutions provided for under these agreements are similar to those of the Yaounde Association, as outlined previously. Councils of the Association, composed of members of the EEC organs and of members of the Greek or Turkish governments, have an element of supranationality, and may take decisions binding on all partners. These Councils have established Association Committees to ensure the smooth operation of the agreements. In addition, Parliamentary Association Committees have been set up as advisory bodies composed of an equal number of deputies from the European Assembly and from the Greek or the Turkish Parliament.

Morocco and Tunisia

The Maghreb* countries have had historical ties with Spain, France, and Italy for many centuries. Subsequently, Morocco and Tunisia became French Protectorates, while Algeria became part of France. The former countries acquired independence in 1956, and Algeria in 1962, after an eight-year war.

Agreements with Morocco and Tunisia were signed in 1969, establishing "partial" association, in the sense that they do not contain provisions for financial aid and for the free movement of labor. The Six have undertaken to remove customs duties and quotas on most industrial exports and to grant preferences on agricultural products from these countries. The main problem of this Association is the competitive aspect of their farm products. Not only do their exports of fruit, vegetables, and wine compete with French and Italian goods, but Maghreb oranges also compete with those from the Lebanon and Israel, with whom the EEC entered into trade agreements in 1964.

---

*Maghreb is an Arab word meaning "west" and the term is used to describe the western part of the Arab-speaking world, that is, Morocco, Algeria, and Tunisia.

Algeria

Political differences have hampered association with Algeria. Algeria was originally due to participate in the Community's negotiations with Morocco and Tunisia, but its declaration of war on Israel in 1967 provoked a veto from the Netherlands.[6] Recently, this veto has been lifted, and negotiations are proceeding. In the meantime, Algerian wine enters the Community with a 40 percent reduction of the common external tariff.

Malta

An association agreement providing for customs union between the EEC and Malta was signed in 1970, mainly for industrial products. As Malta benefits from the Commonwealth Preferential system, she will have to give the Community treatment at least as favorable as she gives to the United Kingdom, by the end of the first five years. The prime minister of Malta has recently asked for a revision of the agreement to include financial aid and agriculture.

Cyprus

The association agreement with Cyprus was signed in 1972, and came into effect in February 1973. The agreement aims at removing virtually all trade barriers between Cyprus and the Nine, over a period of nine and one-half years. The EEC makes an immediate tariff cut of 70 percent on industrial goods (except petroleum products), while Cyprus reduces her tariffs by 35 percent over four years. The main problem was sherry exports to Britain and Ireland: Cyprus will be given two years' grace before full application of the common agricultural policy.[7]

Africa

Nigeria

In 1966, the Lagos Convention was signed by the EEC and Nigeria. This was a turning point in the development of the Association System. For the first time, a country without political or historical ties with the Common Market entered into association with the Community. Moreover, this was a Commonwealth, English-speaking country. The main reason behind this move was the substantial trade that Nigeria carried out with some members of the EEC. Nevertheless, it was a bold step for a Commonwealth country to take, especially after the breakdown of the first British negotiations for entry.[8] The significance of the Association with Commonwealth countries will be examined in Chapter 3.

Similarly to other association agreements sui generis, the terms of the Lagos Convention were more limited than those of Yaounde. Institutional links were kept to a minimum, and Nigeria did not ask for financial aid.

> Nigeria's rejection of assistance from the EEC overseas Fund or of any financial co-operation with the Community (although she accepted aid from the member states on a bilateral basis) served to demonstrate that an association agreement could cover the trade needs of a developing country without tying the country to multilateral aid and, therefore, multipolitical pressure.[9]

The EEC gave duty-free entry quotas to Nigeria's most important exports (palm products, cocoa, tropical timber, and groundnut oil), whereas the Yaounde associates were given unlimited free entry into the Common Market. In return, Nigeria dropped customs duties on 26 items from the Six, which accounted for only 4 percent of her total imports.

The Lagos Convention never came into effect, however, due to the civil war that ravaged Nigeria later that year. As was shown above, under the section on the Lomé Convention, Nigeria was one of the signatories of the 1975 agreement and is thus now a full associate of the EEC.

Kenya, Tanzania, Uganda

Following in the footsteps of Nigeria, these three East African countries became associates of the EEC by the Arusha Convention of 1968, renewed in 1969, at the same time as Yaounde II. The Arusha agreement provided for substantial liberalization of EEC imports from Kenya, Tanzania, and Uganda, and duty-free quotas for coffee, cloves, and tinned pineapples. In return, the associates granted preferences of between 2 percent and 9 percent on a group of about 59 EEC products. The Arusha agreement was replaced by the Lomé Convention of 1975, to which Kenya, Tanzania, and Uganda are signatories.

TRADE AGREEMENTS

Besides association agreements, the EEC has signed a number of trade agreements with third countries, mainly in the Mediterranean area. This is to cover cases where countries wish to make some commercial arrangement with the EEC, but prefer not to become too closely linked with the Community.

Iran

In October 1963, Iran entered into a trade agreement with the EEC, in order to protect the exports of a number of products to the Common Market, especially rugs, raisins, dried apricots, and sturgeon caviar. The agreement covers tariff reductions of 10 to 20 percent and other concessions. (Greece, associated since 1961, was upset by the concession regarding raisins, which compete with Greek exports). A Joint Committee consisting of EEC and Iranian officials was established to attend to the implementation of the agreement.

Israel

For several years, Israel has been seeking a formal relationship with the EEC, but negotiations have been slow and difficult for economic and political reasons. Inter alia, Israel exports compete with Italian products, especially citrus fruit. A trade agreement dating from 1964 was renegotiated in 1970, but in the meantime Israel has applied for associate status, and the Six have viewed their talks with this country as part of the Community's relations with the Middle East.

Lebanon

A trade agreement between Lebanon and the EEC was signed in May 1965. Tariff reductions were not included, but the agreement concentrated on the mutual extension of most-favored-treatment, including nontariff obstacles and technical assistance. In 1972, a preferential agreement was signed, covering 58 percent of Lebanon's industrial exports to the Community and almost 40 percent of its farm exports. As in the Israeli agreement, a Joint Committee has been provided for, to supervise the running of the agreement.

Yugoslavia

A three-year, nonpreferential trade agreement was signed in 1970. This is the first agreement between the EEC and an East European country.

Spain

Although Spain has expressed interest in the Association, there has been opposition from the Benelux countries toward anything that could be construed as giving political approval to the Spanish government. As a compromise, a trade agreement between Spain and the EEC was signed in 1970, liberalizing trade on both sides for a period of six years. This will benefit over 95 percent of Spain's industrial exports and 62 percent of its agricultural exports to the Six, and 61 percent of the Community's total exports to Spain.[10]

Egypt

Egypt and the EEC signed their first five-year trade agreement in December 1972. It provides for a tariff cut of 55 percent by the EEC on imports from Egypt, but quotas restrictions will remain on petroleum and cotton products. There will also be significant concessions in the agricultural sector. In return, Egypt will grant tariff concessions on industrial imports from the EEC.

Argentina

In November 1971, the Common Market signed a trade agreement with Argentina, the first Latin American country to establish formal links with the Community. The three-year, nonpreferential treaty reduced restrictions on imports to the EEC of beef and veal (Argentina's main products) and encouraged exports of manufactures from both sides. The arrangement also set up a joint commission for consultation on commercial and economic matters. This agreement acted as a model for agreements with other Latin American states.[11]

Uruguay and Brazil

Nonpreferential trade agreements were signed in 1973 for a period of three years.

Several other trade agreements have been entered into between the EEC and certain countries for specific products such as handicrafts, textiles, jute, and coconut products: Bangladesh, India, Pakistan, Thailand, Philippines, Indonesia, and Sri Lanka (1968-74).[12]

EFTA Countries

Until recently, most members of the Association System were developing countries. A new development is the formation of a free-trade area with those members of EFTA that did not join the EEC. Sweden, Norway, Finland, Switzerland, Austria, Portugal, and Iceland have all entered into trade agreements with the enlarged Community to avoid raising tariffs between EFTA countries and the new EEC members, Britain and Denmark. Apart from a few sensitive products such as paper, the new arrangements created free trade in industrial products between 16 countries of Europe.

CRITICISMS OF THE ASSOCIATION SYSTEM

Many countries reacted adversely to the establishment of the Association System, both in 1957 and since the Yaounde Convention of 1963. Reasons varied. In some cases, criticisms came from developing nations which feared that their trade with the EEC would suffer due to their exclusion from the preferential treatment given to associates. More general criticisms were that the Association divided Africa into two groups, associates and nonassociates, and that since it created a new preferential area, it infringed the rules of the GATT. Moreover, it was alleged that the Association is a form of neocolonialism, while some writers have attacked the system because it has failed to develop the associated countries. These criticisms will be examined briefly below.

The most serious allegation is undoubtedly that the Association would cause damage to the external trade of nonassociates, while exports of associates to the EEC would benefit from the trade arrangements with the Community. Obviously, associates hoped that a free-trade area with the EEC would expand their exports to the Community. Protagonists of the Association assumed that this would occur without a reduction of the trade between the EEC and other developing countries, but simply because of the Community's economic growth. Trade figures for associates and nonassociates will be compared in Chapter 4 to assess the validity of these arguments.

It is true that during the Yaounde Convention 1963–75, Africa could be divided into associates and nonassociates but this was certainly not a new division. Since the "scramble for Africa" in the nineteenth century, Africa has been divided, mainly into French-speaking and English-speaking Africa, and more recently into Commonwealth and non-Commonwealth countries. But, as will be outlined in the next chapter, there has been a gradual merging of the two systems and the Lomé Convention has shown that, in the framework of their relationship with the EEC, both Francophone and Anglophone, Commonwealth and non-Commonwealth countries have become a united bloc. The main differences that result from their contact with different European traditions and languages will doubtless remain for the foreseeable future, but is not the consequence of the EEC Association System.

The conflict between association and trade agreements and the GATT rules is a lasting problem. The basic cause of the conflict may be attributed to the dual nature of regional arrangements: freer trade between the parties involved, and discrimination against third parties. Although in some cases agreements establish customs unions (for example, Spain, Malta), most of them were based on the principle of free-trade areas until the 1975 Lomé

Convention. The elimination of reciprocity in tariff concessions undermines the proposition that the new arrangements lead to free-trade areas, but this was done at the request of the associates and other countries. The attitude of the GATT to preferential arrangements will be examined in Chapter 6.

If the term "neocolonialism" is taken in a broad sense to mean a certain dependence on the EEC on the part of associates, then the allegation that the system is a form of neocolonialism may be defended. In that case, any kind of aid to the Third World may be regarded as neocolonialism. On the other hand, if the term is defined as the perpetuation of colonial status, there is no evidence of this in the Yaounde and Lomé Conventions, which underline the equality of status of the signatories. "To regard association as a manifestation of collective neo-colonialism in its pejorative aspects, wholly misinterprets both its conception and functions."[13]

Finally, the Association System was never meant to be a magic formula that would develop the economies of associates in a few years. Trade and aid arrangements between those countries and European Community may help, but it is well known that development problems are vast and may remain unsolved, at least in the foreseeable future.

This review of association and trade agreements illustrates the diversity of a system that links industrialized Western nations to ex-dependencies, Commonwealth countries, and nations with no historical ties with the European Community. Bearing in mind the various forms of economic integration, the Association System as a whole does not fit very clearly into any of the categories listed in the previous chapter. The first Association (1957) established one large free-trade area between the Community and dependencies of its members, the Yaounde Conventions set up 18 free-trade areas between the EEC and each of the associates, but the Lomé Convention leads to free-trade areas only where the most-favored-nation treatment accorded by an associate to EEC products is duty-free. Where this is not the case, it is cooperation rather than integration, since the EEC is giving preferential treatment to exports from associates. This is closely allied to the Generalized System of Preferences and is part of the Community's efforts to establish an overall policy toward the Third World. It must be remembered that the Treaty of Rome does not mention a common policy toward developing countries as a whole. Divergences of national interests in this field—as indeed toward associates—have persisted since 1957 and it is therefore noteworthy that in spite of these difficulties, the nine members of the EEC have undertaken the commitments outlined in the Lomé Convention and other agreements.

NOTES

1. See J. Matthews, "Free Trade and the Congo Basin Treaties," *South African Journal of Economics* 27, no. 4 (December 1959): 293–300.

2. Werner Feld, *The European Common Market and the World* (Englewood Cliffs, N.J.: Prentice-Hall, 1967), p. 115.

3. Feld, *The European Common Market and the World,* p. 115.

4. "Lomé Dossier," *The Courier* (Brussels, Commission of the European Communities), no. 31 (Special Issue, March 1975), p. 38.

5. See Feld, *The European Common Market and the World,* pp. 59–69.

6. *European Community,* September 1970, p. 13

7. *European Community,* February 1973, p. 26.

8. For details on Nigeria's position, see P.N.C. Okigbo, *Africa and the Common Market* (London: Longmans, 1967).

9. P.N.C. Okigbo, *Africa and the Common Market,* p. 132.

10. See *European Community,* September 1970, p. 10.

11. See *European Community,* December 1971, p. 6.

12. *European Community,* June and July/August 1974.

13. Carol Ann Cosgrove and Kenneth J. Twichett, "The Second Yaounde Convention in Perspective," *International Relations* 3, no. 9 (May 1970): 686.

CHAPTER

3

THE ASSOCIATION-COMMONWEALTH CONVERGENCE

The Association System of the EEC was planned to deal with the relationship between Common Market countries and their dependencies but it has evolved into a series of agreements between the Community and a number of independent nations. Most of these countries are ex-dependencies of the Nine and are mainly situated in Africa.

Commonwealth associates—countries that are both members of the Commonwealth and associates of the EEC—provide a link between two preferential systems. The purpose of this chapter is to consider the concept that, in Africa, the Association System and the Commonwealth are converging and, therefore, that the Association has an important impact on the trade policies of Commonwealth African nations. Contributory factors of this trend are the similarities of the two systems and recent changes in the pattern of trade of Commonwealth countries in Africa.

COMPARISON BETWEEN THE ASSOCIATION AND THE COMMONWEALTH

Although there are political as well as economic elements in both organizations, the main purpose of this discussion is to consider the trade characteristics of the two systems.

The Association System was described in the previous chapter. Although the development of the Commonwealth is well known, it will be useful to recall the main lines of its evolution.

As British colonies gradually attained independence, a "Commonwealth of Nations" replaced the British Empire. The first territories involved were the so-called "White Dominions," Canada, Australia, New Zealand, South Africa, and Ireland.* Dominion status was given formal recognition by the Statute of Westminster in 1931, but the term "Dominion" fell into disuse after World War II, because of its implication of subordination. Most of the other colonies have since acquired independence and have become members of the Commonwealth, perpetuating the "Crown Link" by recognizing the British monarch as their own. This bond weakened when some members of the Commonwealth became Republics, but they recognize the queen as head of the Commonwealth and as a symbol of the free association of its members.

The Commonwealth is not, strictly speaking, a formal organization, but rather a loose association of independent states. However, as the term "Association" is used here to mean the association with the EEC, the term "organization" will be applied to the Commonwealth.

Thus we see in the evolution of the British Empire into the Commonwealth a gradual weakening of the bonds that originally linked the members of the Empire, but also a recognition of the persistence of common ties. These ties are difficult to define, but they are found "in every sphere—political, economic and cultural. These are the results of history and of a shared association over the years."[1]

The links between members of the Commonwealth are due to a variety of factors, such as a common language, similar traditions in administration and education, similar legal conceptions, migrations of people from one Commonwealth country to another, common interest in sport, and, above all, strong commercial ties, due to years of close trade relations and to the establishment of a preferential system. This last characteristic is the most tangible of these bonds.

The solidarity that exists between members of the Commonwealth is sometimes said to be due to the "Sterling Area." But this is a result, rather than a cause, of the Commonwealth bonds. Moreover, the Sterling Area is not identical to the Commonwealth since it includes non-Commonwealth countries such as Ireland and Iceland, whereas Canada is a Commonwealth state in the dollar zone.

The economic aspect of the Commonwealth is characterized by the system of Commonwealth Preference—sometimes called by its original name, Imperial Preference—which has sustained the strong commercial links between members. This system was established at the Ottawa Conference of 1932, when a number of bilateral trade agreements were signed between pairs of Commonwealth states. According to these agreements, preferential tariffs were to be applied to imports from the signatories. Not all Commonwealth countries were involved, and some countries received preferences from, but did not grant them to, Britain.

---

*South Africa left the Commonwealth in 1961, and Ireland, finally, in 1949.

Similarities

Seven points of resemblance may be distinguished and they are as follows:

1. The origin of both the Association and the Commonwealth is the colonial situation that existed between some members of the EEC and their dependencies, and between Britain and her dependencies. Most British ex-colonies decided to remain in the Commonwealth after gaining independence, perpetuating the cultural and historical links forged by years of contact. Similarly, links persist between France and her former colonies, between Belgium and Zaïre, and so forth. A common language, commercial ties, and similar conceptions of law and education exist in both groups of countries.

2. Accession to the Commonwealth and to the Association is decided freely by independent nations, in spite of the economic dependence of developing nations on their ex-metropolitan area. In the same way as most ex-British colonies admitted the value of the continuation of their links with the Commonwealth and decided to remain within the group, so the Yaounde countries and later, the Lomé signatories postulated that Association with the Common Market would be advantageous to their economies, and entered into an agreement with the Community.

3. Trade is the main element common to both Association and Commonwealth. The most important provision of the Yaounde Convention was the establishment of a free-trade area between the EEC and the associates. In the case of the Lomé Convention, preferential access to EEC markets retains first place. Similarly, the principal advantages of the Commonwealth link are the preferential tariffs applied to goods from Commonwealth countries. In both cases, preferences strengthen commercial ties.

4. There are reciprocal rights and obligations in both systems. Although the benefits given by the Common Market to products from associated countries outweigh the benefits given by these to the EEC, the element of reciprocity preserves the bilateral aspect of the contract. Generally, Commonwealth preferences are also reciprocal, except when debarred by preexisting commitments, such as the Congo Basin Treaties, mentioned in the section on Kenya, Tanzania, and Uganda below (see page 40).

5. In both cases, preferences have been diluted over the years. Commonwealth preference margins have been narrowed by successive GATT negotiations that reduced tariffs on imports from non-Commonwealth countries. In the same way, the extension of Association to new countries reduces the preferential advantages given to the first group of associates, namely the Yaounde countries. The benefits of both the Commonwealth preferential system and the EEC Association will be further reduced by the Generalized System of Preferences.

6. The Yaounde and Lomé Conventions deal with financial and technical cooperation through the European Development Fund and the European

Investment Bank of the EEC. Developing Commonwealth states receive considerable aid from Britain.

7. As mentioned in the last chapter, it is sometimes alleged that the Association System of the EEC has divided Africa in two by separating associates from nonassociates. This criticism does not stand up to scrutiny because prior to the establishment of the Association, Africa was already divided into Commonwealth and non-Commonwealth countries. The root of this goes back to the nineteenth century, when the "partition of Africa" carved the continent into empires for Britain, France, Germany, Belgium, Italy, and Portugal; Germany leaving the field after World War I. The largest groups were the British and French colonies, which evolved into Anglophone and Francophone Africa. Both the Commonwealth and the Association have emphasized certain differences, but they have not created them.

The above-mentioned points have indicated the close resemblance of the Commonwealth preferential system and the EEC Association System. It is, therefore, surprising to recall that several members of the Commonwealth were severely critical of the Association in the early years of its formation, for instance, Ghana.[2]

Differences

There are four major differences between the Association and the Commonwealth:

1. There is a marked diversity between the economies of Commonwealth states. Some are still developing, such as most of the African members, while others, such as Canada, are predominantly developed countries. Some territories are midway between the two, for instance, India. By contrast, most associates are developing areas, at a similar stage of economic development.

2. Article 58 of the Yaounde Convention of 1963 and Article 90 of the Lomé Convention deal with "the request for association with the Community made by a State which has an economic structure and production comparable to those of the Associated States. . . ." Thus the door is left open for other developing countries to enter into Association with the EEC. This is not the case for the Commonwealth. Although no convention was signed regarding membership of the Commonwealth, and therefore no rules were laid down, it is generally accepted that only ex-members of the British Empire are eligible for the status of Commonwealth member, and hence, for the benefits of Commonwealth preferences. The conclusion can thus be drawn that the Association is open to third countries, while the Commonwealth is an exclusive group.

3. As mentioned previously, the Yaounde and Lomé Conventions set up a number of institutions to watch over the application of the provisions of the agreement. In contrast, the only outward evidence of Commonwealth consultation is the occurrence of periodic meetings of Commonwealth prime ministers and the existence of a Commonwealth Relations Office, now incorporated in the Foreign and Commonwealth Office, London. Thus the Association is a more formal type of organization than the Commonwealth.

4. Chronologically, the Commonwealth is a much older structure than the Association. The formal start of the Commonwealth can be attributed to the Statute of Westminster in 1931, although some dominions became independent at a much earlier date. On the other hand, the principle of Association dates from 1957, when the Treaty of Rome was signed by the Six, and was formally agreed to by the associates in 1963.

This difference in time of the initiation of the two systems is particularly important in relation to GATT. When the General Agreement on Tariffs and Trade was signed in 1947, it exempted from the principle of nondiscrimination "certain preferences of long-standing."* This met the special problem of existing preferential arrangements of the Commonwealth, the French Union, and a few others, which the countries involved did not want to abolish. Thus the Commonwealth preferential system is legal under GATT, whereas the Association preferences have evoked considerable criticism from the contracting parties, since they created a new preferential area. This aspect will be examined in greater detail in Chapter 6.

Despite these differences, the EEC Association and the Commonwealth preferential system resemble each other in nature, origin, and purpose. These fundamental similarities have contributed to the growing amalgamation of the two organizations.

CONVERGENCE BETWEEN THE ASSOCIATION AND THE COMMONWEALTH

The nature of the Association-Commonwealth convergence is illustrated by Commonwealth associates, that is, Commonwealth countries that have signed the association agreements with the EEC without leaving the Commonwealth. The first to do so were Nigeria, Kenya, Tanzania, Uganda, Malta, Cyprus, and Mauritius. It is of interest to examine certain aspects of these agreements.

---

*See Appendix E, Article 1 of the GATT.

Nigeria

Although the Lagos Convention of 1966 was not put into effect because of the Nigerian civil war of that year, this agreement has great significance in terms of the principles involved. It represents the first association agreement negotiated between an Anglophone Commonwealth country and the EEC, in spite of objections raised by other members of the Commonwealth and attacks on the Association System, such as that of Dr. Nkrumah: "We have said and will continue to say, that the Common Market is an imperialist device for the collective exploitation of the less developed countries of Africa by the protagonists of neo-colonialism. It must be avoided like the plague."[3]

Nigeria's move was a bold one. It was a departure from a previous nondiscriminatory policy, because although Nigeria benefited from preferences in the British Market, she did not give preferences to imports from Britain or other Commonwealth countries. The origin of this "open-door" policy is the Anglo-French Convention of 1898, which defined British and French spheres of influence in West Africa and gave equal commercial rights to both countries in Nigeria. Although the Treaty lapsed in 1937, Britain did not introduce preferences in Nigeria.

Nigeria's decision to enter into an Association agreement with the EEC was not taken lightly. There were two main reasons. The first was the negotiations between Britain and the Common Market, with all the repercussions that British membership of the EEC would have on Commonwealth trade.

> Between 1958 and 1962, the first serious attempt to build a link between the two blocs [Francophone and Anglophone Africa] stemmed from Britain's application to join the Community. The negotiations that followed had serious implications for Commonwealth African countries and for the future development of intra-African trade.[4]

If at this time, Britain had succeeded in joining the EEC, Nigeria's exports to Britain would have had to meet the common external tariff of the Community, losing her preferential treatment in U.K. markets. By signing an association agreement giving Nigeria certain tariff reductions in the EEC, Nigeria's representatives were compensating for this eventuality, even though the perferences thus established were not equal to preferences lost in Britain.

The other reason was a change in the external trade pattern of Nigeria (see Table 2).

> Expressed as percentages, Nigeria's exports to the EEC increased only very slightly from 34.7 per cent of total exports in 1959 to 36.4 per cent in 1964.

But exports to the United Kingdom fell from over 50 per cent to just under 40 per cent of total exports.[5]

Imports into Nigeria increased in absolute terms from the EEC, and decreased from the U.K., in spite of an overall increase of total imports. These trade figures explain why Nigeria felt it necessary to come to terms with the Common Market.

Having recognized the advisability of some arrangement with the EEC, Nigeria was faced with three choices, accession to the Yaounde Convention in accordance with Article 58, an association agreement sui generis, or a commercial agreement.

Nigeria opted for an association agreement sui generis, and negotiations were followed by the signing of the Lagos Convention in July 1966. This was the first step in the creation of a bridge between the Commonwealth and the Association.

> The Nigerian link between French-speaking and English-speaking Africa *is* important, symbolically and (to a lesser extent) in practical terms of the degree of communication between the major ex-colonial areas of the continent. If Nigeria's accession does no more than break the neo-colonial barrier in the earlier attitudes of the Commonwealth African governments, it will have done a great deal.[6]

As mentioned in the previous chapter, the Lagos agreement never came in force, and Nigeria became a signatory of the Lomé Convention in 1975.

TABLE 2

Nigerian Foreign Trade
(millions of pounds sterling)

	1959	1960	1961	1962	1963	1964
Exports						
Total	161	161	170	164	185	211
U.K.	82	77	77	70	74	81
EEC	56	50	60	57	69	77
Imports						
Total	178	215	216	203	208	254
U.K.	81	91	95	74	71	79
EEC	33	42	44	39	45	59

Sources: Nigerian Trade Summaries: Commonwealth Economic Committee-Commonwealth Trade 1964 and U.K. Board of Trade. Reproduced in P. Uri, ed., *From Commonwealth to Common Market* (Harmondsworth: Penguin, 1968), p. 146.

Kenya, Tanzania, Uganda

Following the precedent established by Nigeria, it was easier for the three East African territories to become associates. The Arusha Convention of 1968 was also a departure from a nondiscriminatory policy. These countries received preferential treatment in British markets but did not grant reciprocal preferences to British goods. The reason for this was the Congo Basin Treaties of 1885 and 1890, which established the "Open Door Policy" in the "Conventional Basin of the Congo," which extends over the East African states.[7] Having acquired independence, however, the East African nations were legally free to alter their commercial policies, since they could not be bound by agreements taken on their behalf by European countries. It was, however, understandably irksome for Britain to see first Nigeria, then East Africa, give to the EEC a preferential treatment that Britain had never received. But Britain was not in a position to complain since she was herself contemplating entry into the Common Market.

Kenya, Tanzania, and Uganda formed the East African Common Market in 1967, but so far,

> practically none of the requirements of a true common market is fulfilled. Yet, the East African Common Market must not be judged as it stands to-day but be seen as it will develop in the long run when the transfer tax and other hampering devices have fulfilled their function of removing existing industrial imbalances.[8]

Talks between the EEC and East African states started in 1963, but almost collapsed in 1966 over disagreement on coffee quotas and the notion of "reciprocal preferences." However, negotiations were reopened and a first agreement was signed in 1968, the Arusha Convention. Since this was not ratified, the Convention was renewed in 1969 and came into effect until it was superseded by the Lomé Convention of 1975, to which the three East African territories are signatories.

The reasons underlying the association agreement between the EEC and East Africa are similar to those of the Nigerian agreement, namely the need to protect these countries' external trade, not only from the consequences of a possible British membership of the Common Market, but also from the results of existing association agreements with countries producing goods similar to those of Kenya, Tanzania, and Uganda.

Malta and Cyprus

The Association agreement between Malta and the EEC (1970) and the agreement with Cyprus (1972) were mentioned in the last chapter. As these countries gave preferential treatment to Britain as members of the Commonwealth, these agreements will simply extend these preferences to other members of the enlarged Community.

Mauritius

The seventh Commonwealth country to become associated with the Common Market is the island of Mauritius (1972). Similarly to the agreements with Malta and Cyprus, this arrangement will eventually give EEC goods the same preferential treatment given to Commonwealth members. The difference is that Mauritius adhered to the Yaounde Convention instead of entering into a sui generis agreement. The links between the EEC and Mauritius were thus closer than between the Community and the East African associates.

The "Associables" and the Lomé Convention

During the negotiations concerning Britain's entry into the EEC, it was decided to offer developing Commonwealth nations some form of relationship with the enlarged Community. These countries became known as the "associables." We have seen that after several years of negotiations, they all became signatories of the Lomé Convention of February 1975, thus doubling the number of associates. It is probable that a large number of African Commonwealth countries would have become associates even if Britain had not entered the EEC, as evidenced by the fact that the Lomé Convention was signed several months before Britain's referendum on the Common Market. The Association System has therefore had a considerable impact on trade policies of Commonwealth developing countries.

By bringing together the two groups, Francophone and Anglophone, the Association has contributed to African unity. Although the old historical division of Africa will persist, the much-criticized division between associates and nonassociates no longer exists in Africa, since the majority of states are now associates of the EEC. It is interesting to note that the extension of Association to so many new countries has not caused a new wave of criticism. Two probable reasons are that the notorious reverse preferences have been abolished and that many of the original critics of the system have become associates.

NOTES

1. *The Future of the Commonwealth: A British View,* "The Report of a Conference Held . . . at the Invitation of the Commonwealth Relations Office . . ." (London: H.M.S.O., 1963), p. 4.

2. Carol Ann Cosgrove, "The EEC and Developing Countries," in *Economic Integration in Europe,* ed. G. R. Denton (London: Weidenfeld, 1969), p. 131.

3. *Ghana Parliamentary Debates,* September 25, 1962.

4. P. N. C. Okigbo, *Africa and the Common Market* (London: Longmans, 1967), p. 70.

5. Dennis Austin, "Britain, Commonwealth Africa and the EEC," in Pierre Uri, ed., *From Commonwealth to Common Market* (Harmondsworth: Penguin, 1968), p. 146.

6. Pierre Uri, ed., *From Commonwealth to Common Market,* p. 158.

7. See J. Matthews, "Free Trade and the Congo Basin Treaties," *South African Journal of Economics* 27, no. 4 (December 1959): 293–300.

8. Ingrid Doimi di Delupis, *The East African Community and Common Market* (London: Longmans, 1970), p. 160. The transfer tax is summarized as follows: "A State which has a trade deficit in its total trade with the other two Partner States may impose transfer tax on manufactured goods originating from the two other States" (p. 83).

4

TRADE BETWEEN
THE EUROPEAN COMMUNITY
AND ASSOCIATES

We have seen that the establishment of the EEC Association System aroused criticism from both developed and developing countries. One of the most important arguments put forward at the time was that the Association would cause trade diversion from nonassociates to associates and would therefore damage the external trade of developing countries not parties to the agreements.

The purpose of this chapter is to consider the impact of the Association System on the trade of the associated countries and to assess the value of the argument that the trade of nonassociates would consequently suffer. The discussion will be conducted under two headings: comparison with nonassociated African countries and comparison with developing countries in other parts of the world.

Statistical data concerning trade between the European Community and associates are limited because recent statistics illustrate the trade between the enlarged Community (EEC-9) and the ACP, whereas an examination of the abovementioned problem requires figures of trade between the Community of the Six (EEC-6) and the original associates, the Yaounde countries (AAMS).

Table 3 shows EEC-6 imports from and exports to African associates and nonassociates. Percentage figures have been rounded to the nearest unit for the overall change and to the nearest decimal for the annual growth rate.

Considering Table 3, EEC-6 imports from the associated African countries have increased by 264 percent (annual growth rate: 8.4 percent) and imports from nonassociated African areas by 930 percent (annual growth rate: 15.7 percent). However, the high figure for imports from nonassociates (10,086 Eur.) is due to increased prices of oil imports and for comparison purposes, the change between 1958 and 1973 has also been considered. For this period, there is a 142 percent increase in imports from associates (6.1 percent annual

TABLE 3

EEC-6 Trade with Africa
(Eur. million*)

Year	EEC-6 Imports		EEC-6 Exports	
	From AAMS	From Nonassociated Developing Countries	To AAMS	To Nonassociated Developing Countries
1958	915	979	714	1,517
1971	1,640	4,225	1,403	2,560
1972	1,717	4,009	1,461	2,889
1973	2,217	4,785	1,669	3,634
1974	3,327	10,086	2,178	5,843
1958–74				
Change	2,412	9,107	1,464	4,326
Percent	+264	+930	+205	+285
Annual growth rate (in percent)	8.4	15.7	7.2	8.8
1958–73				
Change	1,302	3,806	955	2,117
Percent	+142	+389	+134	+140
Annual growth rate (in percent)	6.1	11.2	5.8	6.0

*Unit of account of the EEC = 0.888671 gram of fine gold.
Source: Eurostat, Monthly Statistics, Special number 1958-74 (Luxembourg, Statistical Office of the European Communities), pp. 24-25.

rate) and a 389 percent increase in imports from nonassociates (11.2 percent annual rate).

Turning now to exports from the Community to African countries, the difference between associates and nonassociates is less striking, but once again, the EEC-6 has increased exports to associates to a lesser extent than to nonassociates, for both periods under review.

Table 4 considers the trade between EEC-6 and developing countries as a whole, as well as major developing areas. Again, it is necessary to examine periods 1958–73 and 1958–74 due to the distortion caused by increase in oil prices.

Comparing EEC-6 imports from the AAMS with imports from other regions and from developing countries as a whole, it is noted that the increase is greater for imports from every other major developing area, except Central

TABLE 4

EEC-6 Trade with Major Developing Areas
(Eur. million)

	1958	1973	Percent Change	Percent Annual Growth Rate	1974	Percent Change	Percent Annual Growth Rate
Imports from:							
AAMS	915	2,217	+142	6.1	3,327	+264	8.4
Nonassociation Africa	979	4,785	+389	11.2	10,086	+930	15.7
Central and South America	1,584	4,426	+179	7.1	5,365	+239	7.9
Middle East	1,805	8,078	+348	10.5	20,143	+1,016	16.3
Far East	782	3,022	+286	9.4	4,037	+416	10.8
Other	762	1,277	–	–	1,883	–	–
Total	6,827	23,805	+249	8.7	44,841	+557	12.5
Exports to:							
AAMS	714	1,669	+134	5.8	2,178	+205	7.2
Nonassociation Africa	1,517	3,634	+140	6.0	5,843	+285	8.8
Central and South America	1,531	3,802	+148	6.3	6,155	+302	9.1
Middle East	695	3,268	+370	10.9	5,629	+710	14.0
Far East	1,082	2,727	+152	6.4	3,815	+253	8.2
Other	636	1,811	–	–	2,450	–	–
Total	6,175	16,911	+174	7.0	26,070	+322	9.4

Source: Eurostat, Monthly Statistics, Special number 1958-74 (Luxembourg, Statistical Office of the European Communities), pp. 24-28.

and South America, for 1958–74. Nevertheless, EEC imports from this area have more than tripled.

Turning to exports from the EEC to developing areas, the increase of exports to AAMS is smaller than for every other area, for both periods under review.

Finally, Table 5 calculates EEC-6 trade with the AAMS as a percentage of EEC trade with all developing countries. For imports and exports the share of AAMS trade has dropped from 13.4 percent to 7.4 percent, and from 11.6 percent to 8.4 percent respectively.

TABLE 5

EEC-6 Trade with AAMS Compared to Total Developing Areas
(Eur. million)

	1958	1973	1974
Imports from:			
AAMS	915	2,217	3,327
Developing countries	6,827	23,805	44,841
AAMS as a percent of developing countries	13.4	9.3	7.4
Exports to:			
AAMS	714	1,669	2,178
Developing countries	6,175	16,911	26,070
AAMS as a percent of developing countries	11.6	9.9	8.4

Source: Eurostat, Monthly Statistics, Special number 1958-74 (Luxembourg, Statistical Office of the European Communities), pp. 23-24.

DISCUSSION

This review of EEC trade with developing countries indicates that in the first 16 years (1958–74) of the Association System, there has been no significant trade-diversion from nonassociates to associates. The fear of trade loss by nonassociates is therefore unfounded for the period under review. On the other hand, it is understandable that the associates are disappointed by the results of the trade arrangements of the system, which, under the Yaounde agreements, set up eighteen free-trade areas between the EEC and each associate.

At first sight, it would appear that this proves the validity of customs-union theory, which indicates that the benefits of economic integration are likely to be greater (a) if the economies of the partner countries are actually very competitive but potentially very complementary, and (b) if the amount of trade between them represents a large proportion of their total external trade.[1]

Neither of these propositions hold in the case of the Association System. The products of the EEC and of the associates are complementary, not competitive, except in a few cases, such as fruit, which is excluded from the preferential arrangements. Hence, the elimination of tariffs is unlikely to create new areas of specialization. The proportion of trade between the two groups compared to their total world trade differs; in other words, the bulk of the associates' trade is with the EEC but the share of the EEC trade with associates is small compared with the total external trade of the Common Market.

It would seem, therefore, that according to theory, the actual conditions of the Association System are unlikely to lead to benefits for the countries involved. It would be unwise, however, to draw such a conclusion, for the following reasons:

First, before the establishment of the Association, the associates were already in a preferential arrangement with their metropolitan countries, and in fact, the preferences they received were greater than those given subsequently by the Common Market. For example, in the case of France and her overseas areas, which form the main group of associates, the French customs tariff was higher than the common external tariff applied by the EEC after integration.[2] The associates did not move from a position of free trade to a regional arrangement with the EEC but from one preferential agreement to another. The difference was that the associates exchanged a higher degree of preference in the French market for a lower degree of preference in the wider EEC market.

Second, to suggest that if the conditions mentioned above are not present, the countries concerned should not have integrated, is tantamount to suggesting that the EEC and the ex-colonies of some of the members would have benefitted by applying to each other the same tariffs as they applied to third countries. This would be difficult to accept, when developing countries all over the world are asking developed countries to grant them tariff concessions. Where associates needed to impose customs duties in special circumstances, for revenue or protection purposes, we have seen that the Yaounde agreements allowed them to do so.

Third, the theory of customs unions, as the name implies, concentrates on the effects of customs unions, where a common external tariff is applied, and only marginally on the effects of free-trade areas, where members are free to impose whatever tariffs they wish on imports from third countries. Until the Lomé Convention of 1975, most association and trade agreements established free-trade areas and not customs unions. Since then, there are fewer free-trade areas because the EEC receives only most-favored-nation treatment from the associates, and not free entry.

Fourth, contributions to the extension of customs-union theory to developing countries do not really apply to the Association System since they usually investigate integration among developing areas. Some of the associates have integrated among themselves (the East African associates, the UDEAC countries), but these arrangements do not form part of the Association and are, therefore, outside the scope of this study.

It follows that customs-union theory does not explain the lack of change in the trade patterns of associates, and the question does arise as to what is the cause of this situation. Four factors contributing to this situation are:

1. The Association is fairly recent, and trade liberalization between the European Community and associates was only completed in 1968. Thus it may still be too early to notice any significant effect, since available statistics do not go beyond 1974.

2. Only one-third of the exports of associates are eligible for preferential treatment in the EEC, since the following products enter the Common Market free of tariff, whatever their country of origin: calcium phosphate, gum arabic, ores, crude oil, rubber, raw hides and skins, wood, cotton, sisal, copper, tin, cobalt, tea, seeds, and oleaginous fruits.[3]

3. The margin of preference given to products from associates has been gradually reduced by worldwide lowering of tariffs in conferences of the GATT.

4. Tariff preferences amount to a price advantage, and are not sufficient for an improvement in trade unless they are combined with an increase in production of suitable goods. Unfortunately, the AAMS—and many other developing countries—still export mainly primary products of low price-elasticity of demand.

In an analysis of EEC trade with associates,[4] R. Lawrence concludes that the association arrangements have not had a significant effect on world trade patterns, and he points out that two aspects of the EEC's policies have contributed to this outcome: the reduced preference for some important associate exports (compared to before 1963) and the substitution of capital flows for price-support schemes.

It is also worth mentioning that, although Lawrence refers to the fact that the associates exchanged a higher degree of preference with their ex-metropolis for a lower preference in the larger EEC, he does not explain that the choice facing the associates was not the old arrangement or the new one, but rather Association or isolation. The Treaty of Rome did not permit the continuation of preferential arrangements with individual members of the Common Market.

EFFECTS OF ASSOCIATION

One must agree with Lawrence that the trade of the associates has not greatly improved, and has likewise not caused damage to the EEC trade with nonassociates. Nevertheless, the Association has led to two important changes:

First, the trade of associates with the EEC as a whole has not altered significantly, but the trade with individual members of the Community has changed. Members of the EEC who in the past had no special relations with associates have increased their imports from them at a higher rate than the other members, and, similarly, members without special relations with associates increased their exports to them at a higher annual rate. This is indicated in Table 6.

This shows that the Association, by enlarging the preferential area linked with the associates, has caused an important geographical diversification of both imports and exports of associated countries, which in itself must be considered as a benefit to those countries. Thus, the only noticeable trade-diversion—though not strictly in the Vinerian sense of the term—has been from ex-metropolitan countries to other EEC members, and not from nonassociates to associates.

Second, the other change brought about by the Association System has been the reaction of other countries to this development, which has expressed itself in changes in trade policies, involving a search for similar arrangements with other developed areas, a demand for Generalized Preferences, and a rejection of the nondiscrimination rule of the GATT. These aspects will be discussed later.

TABLE 6

Annual Growth Rate of Trade between EEC Countries and Associates, 1958–74
(in percent)

	Imports from Associates	Exports to Associates
Netherlands	13.4	9.8
West Germany	12.2	12.7
Italy	15.7	13.1
France	5.5	6.3
Belgium-Luxembourg	9.2	3.8

Source: Compiled from Eurostat, Monthly Statistics, Special number 1958-74 (Luxembourg, Statistical Office of the European Communities), p. 24.

It is sometimes alleged that the Association was formed for the benefit of the EEC. However, there is no evidence that the Community has significantly benefitted from the system by expanding exports to the associates. The increase in exports to the AAMS for 1958–74 (205 percent) is less than the increase in exports to developing countries as a whole (322 percent). (See Table 4.) Moreover, the increase in EEC imports from associates (264 percent) is higher than the increase in EEC exports to associates for the same period (205 percent). Thus, EEC purchases from the AAMS have increased more than their sales to the AAMS.

In an article studying the effects of the Association on EEC trade, it is concluded that

> The association arrangement seems to have resulted in trade-diversion, par-
> ticularly against non-associated less-developed countries whose export prod-
> ucts are competitive with those of the Associated African countries.
> However, the extent of trade-diversion was limited owing to various institu-
> tional factors. . . .[5]

One must disagree with the author of this article, because even if the share of nonassociated countries' exports to the EEC had declined compared to the share of associates' exports to the EEC, this is not trade-diversion in the Vinerian sense of the term. To illustrate this point, suppose countries A and B each export 100 units of goods to X. Thus, their share of X's total imports is 50 percent each. Now suppose that in the following ten-year period, A's exports increase to 200 units, while B's exports remain at 100 units. B's share is now one-third, while A's share has risen to two-thirds of the total. However, none of B's trade has been diverted, since X still imports 100 units from B. The only change has been an increase in A's exports to X, and consequently one cannot conclude that this has been trade-diversion from B to A.

Finally, it should be remembered that among writings extending the field of customs-union theory to factors other than production and consumption effects, there is a gradual acceptance that customs unions and similar arrangements are entered into, not only for economic reasons but also for noneconomic reasons. This is the background of the Association System, which attempts to maintain existing links between ex-colonies and European countries.

To assess whether the Association damaged the trade between nonassociates and the Community, we have considered the trade between the Europe of the Six and the 18 Yaounde associates, which were the main groups involved in the system from 1958 to 1974. The picture will change in the future, since the Lomé Convention of 1975 has extended the relationship to a nine-member Community and 46 ACP states, and future trade figures will thus include some Commonwealth trade, that is, trade between Britain and Commonwealth countries. It would be interesting, in a few years' time, to compare EEC-Association trade before and after the Lomé Convention.

NOTES

1. J. E. Meade, *The Theory of Customs Unions* (Amsterdam: North-Holland, 1955), pp. 107–09.

2. Weighted averages—all items: French tariff (1957)—8.1; EEC tariff (1960)—4.8. Weighted averages—preference items: French tariff (1957)—8.7; EEC tariff (1960)—5.1. R. Lawrence, "Primary Products, Preferences and Economic Welfare: The EEC and Africa," in *International Economic Integration,* ed. P. Robson (Harmondsworth: Penguin, 1972), p. 366, Table 1.

3. *Commission of the European Communities,* COM(73) 500/fin. Luxembourg, April 4, 1973. Memorandum . . . on the future relations between the Community, the present AAMS states and the countries in Africa . . ., p. 10.

4. Lawrence, "Primary Products, Preference and Economic Welfare: The EEC and Africa," pp. 362–84.

5. Alassane D. Ouattara, "Trade Effects of the Association of African Countries with the European Economic Community," *International Monetary Fund, Staff Papers* 20, no. 2 (July 1973): 530. (This article contains valuable statistical data, but unfortunately only up to 1968.)

5

**IMPACT OF THE
ASSOCIATION SYSTEM ON
SOUTH AFRICA**

The Association System of the European Economic Community has had an important impact on African trade policies. Most Francophone countries have been associated with the Community since 1957 and the Lomé Convention of 1975 has brought together most independent African states in a unique trade relationship with the EEC.

A survey of the effect of the Association System on Africa would be incomplete without a consideration of the most developed area of this continent, the Republic of South Africa. The Association acts upon the trade policies of South Africa in two ways: first, it offers the possibility of an agreement between the Republic and the Community, which would mitigate the detrimental effects of the loss of tariff preferences in the British Market, and second, it modifies the South African Customs Union, which includes three signatories of the Lomé Convention, namely Botswana, Swaziland, and Lesotho (BSL).

These aspects will be considered in the context of South Africa's trade with Britain and the EEC. This chapter is divided into four parts: an examination of changes in the pattern of South Africa's external trade with Britain and the Community, the effects of Britain's entry into the Common Market, prospect of an agreement between South Africa and the EEC, and, finally, the impact of the Association on the South African Customs Union.

CHANGES IN SOUTH AFRICA'S PATTERN OF TRADE

Table 7 shows South Africa's trade with the EEC, United Kingdom, United States, and Japan as percentages of the Republic's total trade. The years 1958 and 1969 represent trade before and after the establishment of the Com-

TABLE 7

South African Trade with Selected Countries*
(in percent)

	1958	1969	1970	1971	1972
Imports from:					
EEC	18.1	23.7	25.8	24.7	24.8
United Kingdom	33.7	23.7	22.1	23.2	20.9
United States	17.5	17.4	16.7	16.3	16.5
Japan	2.6	8.8	8.7	10.1	9.4
Others	28.1	26.4	26.7	25.7	28.4
Total	100.0	100.0	100.0	100.0	100.0
Exports to:					
EEC	17.1	18.6	18.1	17.7	19.6
United Kingdom	29.8	33.3	29.1	26.7	26.0
United States	7.1	7.1	8.3	7.7	7.2
Japan	1.4	9.9	11.7	11.6	12.7
Others	44.6	31.1	32.8	36.3	34.5
Total	100.0	100.0	100.0	100.0	100.0

*South Africa includes South-West Africa, Botswana, Swaziland, and Lesotho.
Source: Department of Statistics, Republic of South Africa, *South African Statistics,* Pretoria.

mon Market because the Six took ten and a half years to abolish tariffs between themselves.

A comparison between the respective percentages of the EEC and Britain between 1958 and 1972 shows the following changes. For both imports and exports, the share of the EEC has increased and that of Britain, which has always been South Africa's main trading partner, has dropped. Furthermore, a different picture emerges from imports compared with exports. There has been a greater change for imports: South Africa's imports from the EEC increased by 6.7 percent and imports from Britain decreased by 12.8 percent. Changes in exports are much less significant (except for Japan): South Africa's exports to the EEC increased by 2.5 percent during the period under review, while South Africa's exports to Britain decreased by 3.8 percent. Thus, although in 1972 South Africa still exported more to Britain than to the Six, she imported more from the EEC than from Britain.

Considering the figures for Japan and the United States, it is interesting to note that South Africa's trade (both imports and exports) increased proportionately far more with Japan than with the other areas, while the share of the United States remained substantially the same.

Although Table 7 shows trade percentage with the EEC as a whole, Germany is the main trading partner of South Africa, among the Six. In 1971, Germany absorbed almost half of South Africa's exports to the Common Market (265 out of a total of 549 million dollars) and more than half of South Africa's imports from the EEC come from Western Germany (574 out of a total of 1,044 million dollars).[1]

Regarding the establishment of the Common Market on South Africa's trade, her exports to the EEC show a slight increase that may expand in time. The enlargement of the Community, however, will have a dual effect on the trade of the Republic, and the net result will depend on the strength of these divergent trends. South Africa's exports to the Common Market may increase further, if the economy of the Community continues to expand. The enlargement of the group has turned it into the most populated trading group in the world. In 1970, the population of the nine members totaled 253 million, compared to the USSR (243 million) and the United States (205 million).[2] On the other hand, British membership of the EEC may lead to a reduction in South Africa's exports to Britain because South Africa will lose the tariff preferences from which her exports have benefited in the past. This aspect will now be considered in some detail.

EFFECTS OF BRITISH ENTRY INTO THE EEC

On January 1, 1973, Britain, Ireland, and Denmark became members of the European Community. As part of the process of economic integration, the EEC and these countries will abolish all tariffs between them and the new members will apply the common external tariff (CET) of the EEC on imports from outside the Community.

Britain's entry will affect all her trading partners. It will abolish British tariffs on goods from EEC members, reduce them in some cases on goods from non-EEC countries (where the British most-favored-nation rate is higher than the CET) but it will increase tariffs on imports from the Commonwealth, since Britain is moving out of the Commonwealth preferential system.

The transitional phase is planned to last from 1973 to 1977, during which tariffs will be adjusted between Britain and other countries as follows:

EEC Countries Tariffs will be abolished between Britain and the EEC according to the following timetable:

4/1/73	cut of 20%	total adjustment:	20%
1/1/74	cut of 20%	total adjustment:	40%
1/1/75	cut of 20%	total adjustment:	60%

1/1/76   cut of 20%   total adjustment: 80%

7/1/77   cut of 20%   total adjustment: 100%

Non-EEC Countries Britain will adjust her tariffs to the level of the EEC common external tariff toward all third countries. With a few exceptions, this will be done according to the following timetable:

1/1/74   adjustment of 40%   total adjustment: 40%

1/1/75   adjustment of 20%   total adjustment: 60%

1/1/76   adjustment of 20%   total adjustment: 80%

7/1/77   adjustment of 20%   total adjustment: 100%

The direction of these adjustments will differ according to the level of the British tariff toward each third country prior to enlargement. In this regard, a distinction must be drawn between Commonwealth and non-Commonwealth countries, and between EFTA and non-EFTA countries. The South African situation will be examined separately.

Commonwealth Countries

In most cases, these countries have benefitted from preferential treatment for their exports since the Ottawa conference of 1932. By entering the Common Market, Britain has exchanged Commonwealth preference for Community preference and several tariffs will have to be increased from the preferential level to the external tariff.

The problem of Commonwealth preferences was among the more serious difficulties that had to be solved at the time of the negotiations between the United Kingdom and the EEC. Special arrangements were made in the case of New Zealand butter and Caribbean sugar. Developing Commonwealth nations with an economy similar to those of the EEC associates were offered association or trade agreements, and most of them are now parties to the Lomé Convention of 1975. Trade arrangements have been made with India and Pakistan and special treatment is given to products of importance to Sri Lanka (Ceylon) and Hong Kong (for example, a nil duty on tea imports).[3] Australia and Canada will have to adjust their trade to the new situation, as they are not developing countries in need of special arrangements.

It is probable that better terms would have been given to Commonwealth countries if Britain had joined the EEC in 1957. The Association System began as a means of accommodating the special relationship between France and its dependencies, and similar steps could have dealt with the Commonwealth problem. It is not the first time, however, that Commonwealth countries have been at a disadvantage due to changes in the external commercial policies of Britain. The establishment of the European Free Trade Association in 1960 resulted in some cases in the Commonwealth product remaining subject to an import duty—even at a preferential rate—whereas the EFTA product could enter free.[4]

Non-Commonwealth Countries

Among these, EFTA countries were likely to lose their duty-free entry into Britain unless some arrangements could be made. Bilateral agreements between the EEC and those EFTA countries not entering the Common Market have resulted in a 16-nation free-trade zone.[5]

Non-Commonwealth countries that are not EFTA members will benefit from British entry whenever the rate of the common external tariff of the EEC is lower than the British most-favored-nation rate, and will face increased tariffs when the opposite is the case.

South Africa

Although a non-Commonwealth country, the Republic is in a similar position to that of Australia and Canada. The bilateral agreement between Britain and South Africa, signed at Ottawa in 1932, was not conditional on membership of the Commonwealth and therefore was not affected by South Africa leaving the Commonwealth in 1961. Thus the Republic continued to benefit from British preferential tariffs and reciprocally to grant British goods reduction from the most-favored-nation rate. Britain's entry into the EEC led to the abrogation of the 1932 agreement and South Africa's exports to Britain will gradually face the higher CET. The first rise in tariffs will take place on January 1, 1974 and by July 1, 1977, the full CET will have to be met.

Misgivings have been expressed about the possible effects of British entry into the Common Market on the South African export sector. It is not the purpose of this work to examine this problem in detail or to suggest means of marketing and export promotion that should be undertaken to minimize the disadvantages of the new situation.[6] However, the following points must be made.

Together with other countries—Australia, Brazil, Canada, Japan, and New Zealand—South Africa is at present negotiating under Article XXIV (Section 6) of the GATT, for compensation for trade losses resulting from the enlargement of the EEC. This rule provides for compensation for third countries that have lost trading advantages due to the creation or enlargement of customs unions and other forms of economic integration, which is allowed under Article XXIV of the GATT. These compensations usually take the form of tariff concessions, but not necessarily in the same product as those affected by the change.

Any evaluation of the effects of British entry on South African exports must differentiate between industrial and agricultural exports. Industrial tariffs of the EEC are generally lower than those of most other developed areas. A comparison of industrial tariffs after the Kennedy round of the GATT (1964–67) revealed in the following figures in unweighted averages:[7]

EEC	7.6%
U.S.	11.2%
UK (most-favored-nation)	10.2%
(preferential)	1.2%
Japan	9.8%

Thus, although South African industrial exports will face higher tariffs than previously, these are still relatively low.

The prospect is different with regard to South Africa's agricultural exports to Britain. Agriculture in the Common Market is protected by the common agricultural policy (CAP), which results in the application of levies on imports, in order to bring the prices of imports to the level of domestic prices. In some cases, agricultural imports have to pay the common external tariff as well. The CAP supports high food prices within the Community, to enable persons engaged in the agricultural sector to earn incomes comparable to those in other sectors of the economy.

The South African industries most likely to suffer a setback when Britain increases tariffs to the CET level are fruit, vegetables, and wine. Next to diamonds, this group is the main export to the United Kingdom. Various steps can be taken to minimize the drawbacks, apart from requests for compensation through the GATT, mentioned above. Regarding the wine industry, South African products can avoid paying the full amount of the CET by conforming to the EEC rules of origin ("appellation originée").* Fresh fruit and vegetables may be able to benefit from seasonal advantages and it must be remembered that the Republic has an established market for oranges in the Community. Greater efficiency in local industries and improved marketing and advertising may help these industries to retain their present place in the British market.

---

*This requires specific reference to quality and guaranteed genuineness of product in respect of area, vintage, and so forth.

South Africa may benefit in the long run from the probable improvement in the British economy due to its membership of the EEC. It is hoped that demand will increase and that British importers will not alter their trade pattern for some time. By then, the Republic may also have expanded its markets in other areas.

The abrogation of the bilateral agreement between South Africa and Britain also affects South African tariffs. The Republic is now free to apply most-favored-nation rates to imports from the United Kingdom, unless these are "bound" under the GATT rules. It is not clear, as yet, which goods will be subjected to these increased rates. South Africa may use this possibility of tariff adjustment as a bargaining tool in future negotiations; for instance, she may offer to maintain a tariff at its present level in exchange for a comparable tariff concession from the EEC.

Finally, the adverse effects of Britain's entry into the EEC on South African trade must not be exaggerated. The Reynders Commission reported it was of the opinion that

> South African producers should . . . generally have no insurmountable difficulty in competing effectively with other countries in the enlarged EEC provided optimum attention is given to such aspects as research, management, processing and infrastructural facilities. . . .[8]

PROSPECT OF AN AGREEMENT BETWEEN SOUTH AFRICA AND THE EEC

South Africa is neither a developing country nor a Commonwealth member. Therefore, she has not been offered special arrangements such as was the case for Commonwealth African countries.[9]

The Yaounde Association was opened to countries "which have an economic structure and production comparable to those of the Associated States" (Article 58) and the Lomé Convention renews this open-door provision in Article 90. But obviously, the Republic's industrial development places her in a different category and she does not qualify for full association.

Special association such as offered by Article 238 of the Rome Treaty offers more scope, since it does not limit the possibility of such an arrangement to developing countries, although so far, most partial associates are developing countries. It was shown in Chapter 2 that the Association System of the EEC has grown far beyond the original institution that was established primarily to deal with problems of the dependencies of EEC members. It now extends to countries with no historical ties with members of the Community, and includes a variety of special association agreements as well as trade agreements. In addition, the enlargement of the EEC has led to arrangements with countries of the Commonwealth not eligible for association (for example, India) while agreements with Israel and Argentina show that the road is open for arrangements with semideveloped areas or, to use a term of the Reynders Commission, "middle-zone" countries.[10]

Although the possibility of an association agreement between South Africa and the EEC cannot be excluded, the real problem lies in the political sphere. Most countries are prepared to trade with South Africa, but they are reluctant to enter into a closer relationship because of the Republic's policy of apartheid. African associates, in particular, object strongly to any suggestions that an arrangement could be worked out with South Africa. In this respect, the case of Spain and Portugal is of special interest. For many years, an agreement with those countries seemed impossible due to their undemocratic political systems. Yet, in 1970, a trade agreement was signed with Spain, establishing a customs union with the EEC, and as Portugal is a member of EFTA, she qualified for those trade arrangements that the EEC made with EFTA members following the enlargement of the Community, even before the recent change in Portuguese government. Thus it must be pointed out that political opinions change and that the possibility of an association agreement must not be rejected out of hand.

Nevertheless, a trade agreement between South Africa and the EEC appears to be the most feasible solution. The Republic may prefer this arrangement to a closer relationship, such as an association agreement. It must be borne in mind, however, that under the rules of the GATT, any tariff concession must be extended to all members of the GATT on a most-favored-nation basis. The Republic could ask for better terms for exports of fruit, vegetables, and wine, and offer in exchange tariff concessions on imports of industrial goods from the EEC. South Africa could make use of the bargaining tool mentioned above and offer to maintain the preferential tariffs applied to British goods and extend these, or some of them, to similar products from the whole Community, since the abrogation of the bilateral agreement with Britain leaves South Africa free to adjust those tariffs to the most-favored-nation rate. Presumably, this move would obtain British support within the EEC, as British exporters would not wish to lose those favorable terms in the South African market.

THE SOUTH AFRICAN CUSTOMS UNION

Since 1910, a customs union has existed between South Africa and the three neighboring territories, now the independent states of Botswana, Swaziland, and Lesotho (BSL). The customs revenue is divided according to a specific formula, providing a substantial source of revenue to the smaller territories. It is also a monetary union, since BSL use either the South African rand or a linked currency, although changes are pending in this respect.

BSL have now joined the Association of the EEC by signing the Lomé Convention of 1975. This means a change in the provisions of the customs union, since EEC goods should benefit from most-favored-nation treatment in BSL and vice versa, many BLS goods will enter the EEC duty-free. Rules of origin will have to be worked out to deal with the problem of reexport from BSL.

A closely allied problem is that of the Transkei, which is due to achieve independence in October 1976 under the separate development policy of the South African government. It is expected that the Transkei will become a member of the South African Customs Union but its eligibility to the Lomé agreement depends on international recognition of its independent status, which is in doubt at present.

CONCLUSION

Although South Africa is trading gradually less with Britain and more with the Community, Britain remains South Africa's main trade partner. British entry into the Common Market and the fact that the South African Customs Union is affected by the Lomé Convention have increased South Africa's chances of an arrangement with the EEC, since "the Community does not preclude individual negotiations with aggrieved parties who can show that enlargement harms their trade."[11] A trade agreement between the EEC and the Republic would bring her into the Association System but there will have to be a change in the internal policies of the country before this can come about.

NOTES

1. European Economic Community, European Statistical Office, *Foreign Trade Statistics,* Brussels, 1972, no. 2, pp. 34 and 36.

2. Extracted from *Basic Statistics of the Community,* Luxembourg, Statistical Office of the European Communities, 1971.

3. Dennis Swann, *The Economics of the Common Market,* 2d ed. (London: Penguin Modern Economics Texts, 1972), p. 184.

4. *Commonwealth Preference* R.5155/69 (London: British Information Service, 1969), p. 14.

5. *European Community,* September 1972, p. 11. (See also Chapter 8 herein.)

6. See inter alia, J. J. Williams, *The Competitive Situation for South Africa* (South African Foreign Trade Organization [SAFTO], 1971) and C.J.A. Wright, "The Probable Effects of Bri-

tain's Entry into the EEC on the Economy of South Africa," *The South African Banker* 70, no. 2 (May 1973): 123–30.

7. H. G. Johnson, ed., *New Trade Strategy for the World Economy* (London: G. Allen and Unwin, 1969), p. 206. These are "nominal" rates. It has been shown that "effective" rates of protection are often higher than the "nominal" rate. See John Pincus, *Trade, Aid and Development* (New York: McGraw-Hill, 1967), pp. 189–90.

8. Republic of South Africa, *Report of the Commission of Inquiry into the Export Trade of the Republic of South Africa,* RP 69/72. Government Printer, Pretoria, 1972, p. 89.

9. See J. Matthews, "Prospect of an Association Agreement between South Africa and the European Economic Community," *South African Journal of Economics* 38, no. 2 (June 1970): 152–62.

10. "South Africa, Canada, Australia and New Zealand claim themselves to be 'middle-zone' countries, i.e. neither fully industrialised nor developing countries, on the grounds that they are still heavily dependent on exports of primary products while importing manufactures for purposes of industrialisation." *Report of the Commission of Inquiry into the Export Trade of the Republic of South Africa,* p. 60.

11. *European Community,* February 1973, p. 12.

6

THE GENERAL AGREEMENT ON TARIFFS AND TRADE, AND PREFERENCES

The first part of this book examined the Association System of the EEC and the impact of this development on Africa. The influence of the Association System on more general aspects of international economic relations will now be discussed.

This chapter details the position of the GATT toward tariff preferences and, more specifically, toward the preference embodied in the EEC association and trade agreements, which have caused, and are still causing, considerable controversy.

The General Agreement on Tariffs and Trade, signed in 1947 by 23 countries, was meant to be an interim measure in the formation of a more ambitious plan, the International Trade Organization. However, the United States failed to ratify the Havana Charter of the ITO and the scheme was abandoned, leaving the GATT as the only viable undertaking.

The main purpose of the General Agreement, which consists of a set of rules for international trade, is to liberalize trade by a progressive reduction of tariffs. The GATT acts by pressure and persuasion since it has no power of coercion on its members. In the last 28 years, 60 countries have joined the GATT, bringing the total number of Contracting Parties to 83, while a few others have acceded provisionally. The GATT headquarters and general secretariat are situated in Geneva, Switzerland, where most of the "rounds" of negotiations take place, the latest being the current Tokyo round.

Article I of the GATT explicitly rejects preferences by declaring that, "trade shall be conducted in a non-discriminatory manner, on the general basis of equality of treatment for all Contracting Parties."* Although exceptions

---

*See Appendix E for relevant articles of the GATT.

have been allowed, the GATT has on many occasions reaffirmed its belief in its unconditional most-favored-nation clause, but has been unable to prevent an increase of preferential arrangements.

The GATT considers two types of preferences in tariff matters. One is unilateral, and when tariff concessions are made, the rule is that the preference should be extended to all Contracting Parties. Mutual preferences, on the other hand, are those inherent in the formation of free-trade areas or customs unions and are only allowed by the GATT according to the conditions laid down in Article XXIV. One of the conditions is that the reciprocal elimination of tariffs will involve "substantially all the trade" between members of the free-trade area or customs union.*

A consideration of the benefits that tariff preferences may have on the economies of developing countries and on world welfare as a whole, is beyond the scope of this book.† The only concern here is with the conflict between the Association System and the principles of the GATT, and with the impact of this conflict on the rules of the GATT.

This chapter will therefore outline the views of the GATT at the signing of the General Agreement in 1947, preferential agreements that have taken place since then, the specific problem of preferences contained in EEC association and trade agreements, and finally, some comments on possible changes in the GATT rules on this matter.

EARLY VIEWS OF THE GENERAL AGREEMENT ON TARIFFS AND TRADE

During the discussions leading to the establishment of the GATT, two conflicting attitudes toward preferences became evident, as shown in the viewpoints of the United States and Britain. This duality still exists today among the international commercial policies of the GATT members.

The viewpoint of the United States, which was the prime mover of the GATT, was that preferences should be discarded and that trade should be conducted in a nondiscriminatory manner. "The United States had made elimination of all preferences a major principle of its policy for the post-war organisation of world trade. The chief goal of the U.S. policy was elimination of the Imperial preference system established at the Ottawa Conference of 1932."[1]

The United Kingdom, on the other hand, had no wish to dismantle the system of Commonwealth preferences, which had formed part of the British

---

*See Appendix E for relevant articles of the GATT.

†The advantages and disadvantages of Generalized Preferences (given by developed countries to manufactured exports from developing countries) will be examined in Chapter 7.

commercial policy for many years. Most countries appeared to align themselves with one or the other viewpoint, not on theoretical grounds, but according to whether they were part of a regional arrangement or not. The Scandinavian countries, which at that time did not belong to any economic regional group, sided with the U.S. point of view, whereas France, as part of the Franc zone whose preferential arrangements go back to 1928, agreed with Britain for the retention of these preferences.

The Principle of Nondiscrimination

The results of the duality of positions on preferences was embodied in Article I, which reads:

1. With respect of customs duties, any advantage granted by any Contracting Party shall be accorded immediately and unconditionally to the like product originating from all other Contracting Parties.
2. The provisions of paragraph 1 of this article shall not require the elimination of any preferences which fall within the following descriptions. . . .

There followed a list of existing preferences, including the Commonwealth preferences, those of the French Union, Benelux, and so forth. These were allowed to remain provided that the margin of preference did not increase.

Thus the first article of the GATT embodied the principle of nondiscrimination and the exceptions. It may also be said that Article I included both the theory and the practice, or the ideal and the reality. "The effect of seeking to outlaw preferences was, ironically enough, to write a permanent exemption into the General Agreement for most existing preferential systems."[2]

It is of interest to note that among the exceptions to the rule were the preferential arrangements between the United States and Cuba, and between the United States and the Philippines, although the United States had an official nondiscriminatory commercial policy.

By exempting existing preferences from the rule of nondiscrimination, the General Agreement undermined the principle of equality of treatment for all Contracting Parties. Furthermore, by differentiating between preferences existing in 1947, and those which may be set up later, accepting the first and forbidding the others, the Agreement became the defender of the status quo in commercial policies. This was especially a handicap for countries that acquired independence in the years following the establishment of the GATT, a great number of which became parties to the General Agreement. Those countries that did not already belong to a preferential area, and wished to do so, found that this was prohibited by Article I of the GATT.

The view that existing preferences should be allowed to remain, but that new ones should be discouraged, is vulnerable to criticism. If preferences are detrimental to international trade, then those existing in 1947 should have been gradually dismantled over a reasonable period of time.

The exemption for existing preferences is not the only exception to the rule of nondiscrimination. It will be shown in Chapter 8 that there are other reasons for the weakness of the GATT's first principle. The only other exception relevant here is Article XXIV, because this was invoked by the EEC in order to enter into association agreements with other countries.

The Principle of Reciprocity

One of the main rules of the GATT is that concessions in tariff and other customs matters should be carried out on a reciprocal and mutually advantageous basis (Article XXVIII bis). This means that contracting parties need only make concessions when they are offered similar concessions by other members. The expression "mutually advantageous" is not explicit, and the fact that reciprocity is not defined in the General Agreement leaves the way open for a variety of interpretations.

Although the principle of reciprocity was generally acceptable when the Contracting Parties were mostly developed countries, it soon became evident that it needed revision when the number of developing members of the GATT increased considerably. This was done in 1965, when a new chapter was added to the Agreement, to provide for the special requirements of developing members. In this new section of the GATT, Article XXXVI (8) reads: "The developed Contracting Parties do not expect reciprocity for commitments made by them in trade negotiations to reduce or remove tariffs and other barriers to the trade of less-developed Contracting Parties." Thus the GATT rejects "reverse preferences" from developing to developed countries, because they are thought to be inconsistent with the development needs of those countries. This aspect was one of the reasons for the criticism leveled at some of the EEC Association agreements with developing countries, as discussed below.

PREFERENTIAL AGREEMENTS SINCE 1947

Before examining the case of the Association System of the European Economic Community, and the infringement of the GATT rules that it is alleged to entail, it is of interest to mention briefly four preferential agreements that were condoned by the GATT, through the granting of a waiver:[3]

As early as 1948, the United States asked the GATT permission to give preferential treatment to imports from Pacific islands under U.S. trusteeship.* The reason offered was that these islands had been under Japanese mandate and had received preferential treatment from Japan, and that duty-free access to the U.S. market would compensate the islands for the loss of the Japanese preferences and thus help their export earnings and their economic development. Although Japan had reverse preferences in these Pacific islands, the United States did not seek this. The request was granted in the form of a waiver of the United States' nondiscriminatory commitments. There was some fear that this would create a dangerous precedent, however, and the Contracting Parties reserved the right to review the situation if injury to the trade of other members ensued from the preferences. It appears that no such request has been made so far, probably because the preferences covered only a small portion of trade, namely coconut oil and copra.

The second preferential arrangement allowed by the GATT was that between Italy and Libya in 1951. A waiver was granted to Italy so that she could continue to give preferential treatment to a number of products from Libya. This could be regarded as a technical matter, however, because Libya had received preferential treatment from Italy as a colony. The change in status brought about by its independence made it necessary for Italy to ask the GATT for a waiver, which was duly granted under certain conditions.

In 1953, Australia asked for a waiver of its most-favored-nation obligations in order to grant duty-free entry to goods from the territory of Papua-New Guinea. Reverse preferences were not to be applied, although the possibility of incorporating the area in question into the Australian customs territory was investigated and rejected. Contracting parties were worried about the fact that the goods subject to preferential treatment were not listed. The main reason for the Australian request was once again that this would help the economic development of Papua-New Guinea and the waiver was granted.

These first three preferential agreements condoned by the GATT resulted in a certain awareness of the need for a change in the GATT rule in order to provide a guiding principle for similar cases in the future. In 1954, the United Kingdom proposed that a new rule be added to the Agreement to enable metropolitan countries to give preferential treatment to a dependent territory without breaking the GATT rules. This could be done by regarding the territory as being in the same customs area as the metropolitan country. The contracting parties rejected the British proposal for the following reasons. First, there was the concern of another breach of the nondiscriminatory rule,

---

*The Marshall, Caroline, and Marianas Islands, except Guam.

and of the principle that no new preferences should be allowed. This concern was felt by developed countries which at that time enjoyed no preferences but were soon to form the European Free Trade Association, inter alia Switzerland and Sweden. Second, some members feared that this new proposal would threaten their own exports if they did not seek preferences for themselves. Third, there was a fear that it would perpetuate the dependence of the territory on the metropolitan country.

The search for a formula to give preferential treatment to exports from developing countries was to lead, nine years later, to the "Brasseur plan," which suggested the first steps of the Generalized System of Preferences. This will be discussed in the next chapter.

A more recent breach of the nondiscrimination rule and perhaps the most surprising because it emanated from countries that are both highly developed and were the most prominent defenders of the GATT rule, was the United States-Canadian Automotive Products agreement of 1965. According to this arrangement, tariffs on most automotive vehicles and original equipment parts were to be eliminated between the two countries. Canada planned to extend this tariff cut to imports from other countries, but the United States had no intention to do likewise.[4]

PREFERENCES IN THE EEC ASSOCIATION AND TRADE AGREEMENTS

From the beginning of the European Economic Community, allegations have been made that rules of the GATT were being infringed upon. The calculation of the common external tariff was criticized by a working party of the GATT because the EEC had decided on an arithmetical average of the tariffs of France, Germany, Italy, and Benelux; this system increased tariffs in some cases, and lowered them in others. Although the customs union was permitted by Article XXIV, it was held that the method of calculation contravened the rule that "the duties shall not on the whole be higher or more restrictive than the general incidence of the duties prior to the formation of such union."* The arithmetic average had the great advantage of being a simply method and in spite of representations by the GATT members, the EEC refused to discuss the best method of calculation because they maintained that Article XXIV did not demand any special method, and that their method was appropriate. The underlying reason for this refusal was probably the

---

*See Appendix E for full text of Article XXIV, Sections 4–8.

feeling that unless a definite start was made with the customs union, there was a danger of having every step of the process of integration discussed and delayed by the GATT.

Although the economic union planned by the Six was allowed under Article XXIV, even if the legality of the method of calculation of the common tariff was open to doubt, the Association System was the target of more serious criticism.

The evolution of the Association of African and Malagasy States was traced from Part IV of the Treaty of Rome to the Lomé Convention of 1975 in Chapter 2. The preferences between France and her dependencies, Belgium and the Congo, and so on, are listed in the annexes to the General Agreement and were permitted since they existed prior to 1947. Objections to the Association began, however, when the EEC decided to extend these preferences to other members of the Common Market. Technically, this move constituted the establishment of new preferences. However, the EEC maintained that the Association was creating a new free-trade area including the Six and the Eighteen, and that this was legal under Article XXIV, which reads:

> The provisions of this Agreement shall not prevent the formation of a customs union or of a free-trade area or the adoption of an interim agreement necessary for the formation of a customs union or of a free-trade area.

Several conditions govern the application of this rule, among which is the proviso that customs unions or free-trade areas shall abolish duties and other trade restrictions "on substantially all the trade in products originating in such territories."

Article 133(3) of the Treaty of Rome allows associated countries to levy customs duties in certain circumstances, such as when needed for the protection of infant industries, or for revenue purposes. Contracting Parties of the GATT maintained that this provision prevented the Association from being a true free-trade area, since it did not eliminate tariffs on "substantially all the trade between the parties," and therefore contravened Article XXIV of the GATT.

This objection ignores the fact that the exception contained in Article 133(3) is purely in the interests of the associates, which are all developing countries. It does not nullify the intention to create a free-trade area any more than the omission of agricultural goods from the arrangements of the European Free Trade Association prevents this regional group from being generally accepted as a genuine free-trade area.

In 1957–58, a working party of the GATT considered the terms of the EEC Association, but no final decision was taken except that the Six concluded that "if at any time, contrary to their expectations, damage to the interest of third parties could be proved, the EEC would take steps to mitigate it."[5]

By 1965, the GATT enunciated a new rule regarding the principle of reciprocity that developed countries were not to expect reciprocity from developing countries with regard to tariff concessions.* On these grounds, the GATT and UNCTAD members, and especially developing nonassociated members, challenged the right of the EEC to ask for reciprocity in association agreements with developing countries, that is, to ask for the notorious "reverse" preferences. EEC spokesmen, however, maintain that there are no reverse preferences, only free-trade areas and customs unions.

A free-trade area implies reciprocity in tariff concessions, and therefore, an anomaly appears to exist in the rules of the GATT. Preferential arrangements are allowed only if they lead to the formation of customs unions or free-trade areas, but on the other hand, developed countries should not expect reciprocity from developing countries. Yet without reciprocity, customs unions and free-trade areas cannot be formed. Thus, the GATT would appear to ignore, or object to, the possibility of customs unions or free-trade areas between developed and developing countries.

When the EEC signed the Lagos Convention with Nigeria in 1966, and the Arusha Convention with East Africa in 1968, similar allegations of infringements of the GATT rules were made. With regard to the principle of reciprocity in the Lagos agreement, the Nigerian negotiators considered the problem as follows. Nigeria wanted an agreement similar to that of the Yaounde Convention, but less comprehensive. This included reciprocity in trade concessions since it established a free-trade area. But Nigeria could not offer complete reciprocity in tariff matters and eventually it was decided that the Nigerian preferences offered to the EEC would be nominal.

Following this decision, allegations were made that the free-trade area was fictitious because the concessions offered by Nigeria related to a small portion of Nigeria's trade. But a Nigerian spokesman concluded that "where a preference is created, it is a consequence of, not a condition for, creating a free-trade area, nor can the magnitude of the preference created invalidate the existence of a free-trade area."[6]

The same arguments have been applied to the Arusha Convention, although the preferences given by East Africa to the EEC are somewhat more extensive than in the Lagos Convention.

It is difficult to defend the legality of such association agreements as the Lagos and Arusha Convention under the GATT rules, although the more comprehensive agreement of the Yaounde Convention could have passed the test of Article XXIV. On the other hand, the following aspects must be considered before condemning these agreements.

---

*See Appendix E, Article XXXVI, 8.

Under a free-trade area, there is no common external tariff and therefore associates are free to apply tariffs of their choice to third countries. Thus they could, if they wished, extend the same tariff concessions that they applied to imports from the EEC, to other members of the GATT.

Benefits received by the African countries outweigh those received by the EEC. This is why doubts regarding the legality of these arrangements have not discouraged a number of other nations from becoming signatories of the Lomé Convention, which is a further departure from the principle of a free-trade area, since the EEC receives most-favored-nation treatment from the associates, and not duty-free entry as under the Yaounde Convention.

With regard to trade agreements with the European Community, the early arrangements were nonpreferential. In the agreement with Iran in 1963, for instance, the reduction in the common external tariff of the EEC was extended to other GATT parties, but the products were of interest mainly to Iran: hand-knotted woolen carpets, and so forth. This was also the case with the first agreement between the EEC and Lebanon in 1964. The more recent agreement with Lebanon is preferential and therefore against the GATT rules. The trade agreement with Spain, however, is a customs union (or leading up to a customs union) and does not extend to other countries the tariff reductions between Spain and the EEC.

The official view of the GATT on this matter is not unanimous. Generally, association and trade agreements are deplored: ". . . what is most questionable is the creation of preferential trade links between a few developed and one, or a few, developing countries here and there through new discriminatory agreements for which no historical justification can be claimed."[7] Detailed examination of certain agreements, however, has brought out three tendencies among the GATT members. Some of the contracting parties are of the opinion that the agreements are not inconsistent with the GATT rules, since the declared objective of the parties, the provisions of the agreements and their content, are consistent with the letter and spirit of Article XXIV. Other countries feel the agreements are not consistent with the GATT rules because there is no plan to show how the Association would achieve a full free-trade area or customs union. Finally, some countries make no categorical statement on the compatibility of the agreements with the GATT rules.[8]

The reasons for this divergence of views are often found in the circumstances of the countries expressing these views. For example, it was felt that

if Britain becomes a member of the European Economic Community, there would appear to be no reason, from the point of view of her own interests or those of the developing members of the Commonwealth, why she should not support the continuation of association. . . . If, on the other hand, Britain does not become a member of the European Economic Community, association and other special arrangements . . . are likely to prove disadvantageous

both to her and to the developing countries of the Commonwealth, ...
therefore, it would be in Britain's interest as well as that of the Commonwealth to work for world-wide arrangements.[9]

As will be shown in Chapter 9, sources of conflict in international trade are
frequently due to differences in tariff structure, size of internal market, and
special interests.

THEORETICAL ASPECTS

Customs-union theory has considered specifically the problem of full
preference (as in a customs union) versus partial preference (as in a preferential
agreement).

Jacob Viner points out the illogicality of considering 100 percent preference as good and 99 percent preference as bad. On the legal side, if it is the
degree of preference that makes it contrary to most-favored-nation obligations,
and if customs unions can be regarded as compatible with these obligations,
then preferential agreements, involving a lesser degree of preference, must be
even more so.

> The moral is that on both the economic and legal side the problem is too
> complex to be settled by simple maxims. A 50% preference is economically
> either less desirable or more desirable than a 100% preference according
> only as preference at all is under the circumstances desirable or undesir-
> able.[10]

Nevertheless, Viner singles out one area where partial preference may be
worse than customs unions: the removal of tariff barriers in a customs union
is nonselective, and must lead to both trade-creating and trade-diverting
effects. In the case of preferential agreements, however, they are usually selective, and it is possible and even probable that the preferences selected will be
of the trade-diverting kind.

More recent theories of customs suggest that a partial reduction of duties
on imports from partners is more likely to increase welfare than a complete
removal of restrictions within the area.[11] The reason for this is that the first
reduction of duties within the preferential area contributes to more gain from
trade expansion than each subsequent reduction. On the other hand, the loss
from trade diversion will continue as the degree of preference increases.

This generalization is questioned by Mikesell because

> we are not concerned simply with the readjustment of existing trade pat-
> terns, but rather with alternative principles for the direction of investment
> which will establish the trade and production patterns a decade or so
> hence.[12]

There is, therefore, no consensus of opinion as to whether a full or partial preferential system is more beneficial, in spite of the fact that the GATT accepts the former in Article 24 of the Agreement and disapproves of the latter. This was probably due to the fear that to allow all preferential systems would have opened the door to the bilateralism that plagued international trade in the interwar period. A minor point—but of significance to small countries— is that the administration of a customs union may be more straightforward than selective preferences.

The problem of deciding which type of preference is better stems from the dual aspect of economic integration, a movement toward free trade and simultaneous increase in discrimination. This also explains wide differences of attitudes toward the Association. Some GATT parties regard most Association agreements as discriminatory arrangements resulting in the so-called "reverse preferences." The official view of EEC is expressed as follows:

> The Commission proposes that in respect of trade matters the Association should be based on the principle of the free trade area. The acceptance by the associated states of the mutual free trade area principle does not entail any obligation for them to grant preferences to the Community. They retain complete tariff autonomy in their relations with third countries, and complete freedom to negotiate on such matters.[13]

The Association has also been regarded as "a unique form of development co-operation in that it combines trade and aid under the supervision of special institutions."[14]

RECENT EVOLUTION OF THE GATT'S VIEW ON PREFERENCES

Since the beginnings of the GATT in 1947, the attitude of the contracting parties has undergone a certain change with regard to tariff preferences. We have seen that Article I of the General Agreement condemned new preferences but condoned existing ones. At the same time, the principle of reciprocity in trade matters was upheld.

By 1965, when Part IV was added to the GATT, it was agreed that developing countries should not be asked to reciprocate tariff concessions made by developed countries. This was an acceptance that, in certain cases, preferential treatment is justified. This was reaffirmed in 1971 when a waiver was granted for the establishment of Generalized Preferences in order to promote industrialization in developing areas.*

---

*See Chapter 7.

Thus the main reason for this change in the position of the GATT on preferences was the wish to assist developing countries. There are three other factors, however, that may lead to further alteration in the GATT regulations: the position of the United States in world trade; the movement toward economic integration; and change of emphasis in foreign economic relations.

Although the United States is still the major trader when considered as an individual nation, exports from the EEC as a unit now exceed those of the United States.* Japan is also rapidly becoming one of the giants in world trade. The current multilateral trade talks are being conducted on this new basis, which may affect the GATT regulations since the General Agreement is not an immutable treaty.

> The GATT was founded when the United States was on a pinnacle of pre-eminence. The GATT's rules, of which the most important are reciprocity and non-discrimination, basically enshrined American preconceptions. Now, in trade terms, the balance of power has shifted. It would be surprising if the ground rules, or at least the interpretation of them, did not change.[15]

In addition, the United States drastically affected its position in the GATT when it imposed a surcharge of 10 percent on all imports in August 1971. This was a sudden and unprecedent move on the part of the most important founder of the GATT, and although understandable at the time, due to imperative needs of the U.S. economy, nevertheless it shook the whole concept of the GATT more than any other breach of the General Agreement.

The recent trend toward regional integration may also act upon the GATT's views on preferences. A growing number of countries are forming free-trade areas and common markets in various parts of the world, and several nations are entering into trade agreements with the EEC. The latest group of agreements are those between the EFTA countries and the enlarged Community, which established free trade in Western Europe for industrial goods only. It is doubtful whether this constitutes "substantially all the trade" between the countries involved.†

Due to an increased mobility of other factors of production—labor and capital—the movement of goods and subsequent tariff problems are taking second place in international economics.

---

*In 1970, the United States' total exports were 43,226 million dollars, while the exports of the Six totalled 45,210 million dollars (extra-EEC). The difference will increase with the enlargement of the Community. EEC, Foreign Trade, Monthly Statistics, Brussels.

†This aspect will be considered in more detail in Chapter 8.

Commodity trade has ceased to be the all-important element in foreign economic relations. Capital movements, movements of workers, exchange of know-how, travel, and other services play a fast-growing role and will continue to do so; and, correspondingly, the importance of tariffs and non-tariff barriers to commodity trade is decreasing in the overall picture.[16]

To conclude, association and trade agreements between the EEC and several countries are discriminatory and therefore against the philosophy of the GATT, but since these arrangements are increasing in number, and they result in some trade liberalization, there is a strong possibility that this development will lead to a change in the GATT's views on preferences.

NOTES

1. Kenneth W. Dam. *The GATT Law and International Economic Organization* (Chicago: University of Chicago Press, 1970), p. 42.

2. Ibid., p. 42.

3. For more details, see Gardner Patterson, *Discrimination in International Trade, The Policy Issues, 1945–1965* (Princeton: Princeton University Press, 1966), chapter 7.

4. For more details see Dam, *The GATT Law,* pp. 48–50; and Patterson, *Discrimination in International Trade,* pp. 356–58.

5. W. G. Barnes, *Europe and the Developing World,* PEP European Series No. 2 (London: Chatham House, 1967), p. 13.

6. P. N. C. Okigbo, *Africa and the Common Market* (London: Longmans, 1967), p. 130.

7. General Agreement on Tariffs and Trade, *Press Release,* Address given by Mr. Long, Director-General of the GATT, January 26, 1970, GATT/1051, p. 3.

8. General Agreement on Tariffs and Trade, *GATT Activities in 1970/71* (Geneva, 1972), p. 51.

9. Barnes, *Europe and the Developing World,* p. 46.

10. Jacob Viner, *The Customs Union Issue* (New York: Carnegie Endowment for International Peace, 1950), p. 50.

11. J. E. Meade, *The Theory of Customs Unions* (Amsterdam: North-Holland, 1955), pp. 56 ff.; R. G. Lipsey, "The Theory of Customs Unions: A General Survey," *The Economic Journal* 70, no. 279 (September 1960): 506 ff.; H. G. Johnson, *Money, Trade and Economic Growth* (London: Allen and Unwin, 1962), p. 45.

12. R. F. Mikesell, "The Theory of Common Markets as Applied to Regional Arrangements among Developing Countries," in *International Economic Integration,* ed. P. Robson (Harmondsworth: Penguin, 1972), p. 176.

13. *Commission of the EEC,* "Memorandum of the Commission to the Council on the Future Relations ..." (Luxembourg, 1973), p. 5.

14. R. Cohen, "Europe and Developing Countries," in *The European Community in the World,* ed. Ph. P. Everts (Rotterdam: University Press, 1972), p. 124.

15. *The Economist,* February 28, 1970, p. 65.

16. Günther Harkort, "Response to G. Curzon's Paper," in *Trade and Investment Policies for the Seventies, New Challenges for the Atlantic Area and Japan,* ed. Pierre Uri (New York: Praeger, 1971), p. 69. This view is at variance with the general opinion regarding the importance of nontariff barriers.

7

GENERALIZED
PREFERENCES

The granting of preferences by some countries to a few others has generally been looked upon with distrust and criticism by those not involved in the arrangements. In spite of this, the extension of the Association System of the EEC has had an impact on the attitude of the GATT toward tariff preferences, as was shown in the previous chapter. This trend has been reinforced by a more recent type of preferences, called the Generalized System of Preferences (GSP).

It has been felt for some time that developing countries should be assisted in their efforts to develop their economy. They need to expand their exports in order to purchase imports of consumer and capital goods. So far, most of their exports have been primary products. As returns on these goods are characterized by great instability, some developing countries have been trying to diversify their economies and to export semimanufactured and manufactured goods. In developed countries, tariffs on primary products are usually nil or low, but tariffs on manufactured goods are higher. Moreover, manufactured goods from developing countries have to compete with goods from other industrialized nations. Therefore it has been maintained that assistance should be given—by all developed nations—in the form of preferential tariffs for imports of manufactured and semi-manufactured goods from all developing countries. Although the least developed nations are not likely to benefit a great deal from the GSP since their industrial potential is low, the more advanced among developing countries—for example, Latin American countries—may stand to gain from generalized preferences, especially in the field of semiprocessed agricultural products.

Thus the GSP is meant to redress the balance between developed and developing countries. In particular, it is hoped that it will help the problem of infant industry in the Third World, since preferential tariffs in the markets of developed countries might provide the necessary encouragement to the industries of developing areas, most of which are still at a very early stage of economic development. Local markets in developing countries are unlikely to absorb the optimum output of those industries for some time, and markets abroad are therefore needed for the development of those areas.

The original plan was for all developed countries to give preferential treatment to exports from all developing countries. That is why it is called "generalized" preferences, in opposition to the Association or the Commonwealth preferential systems, which apply only between some developed and some developing countries. As will be shown in this chapter, the plan that was finally accepted was for each developed country to apply its own GSP to all developing countries.

The Association System of the EEC has played a part in the establishment of the GSP. Although the first requests for tariff preferences for manufactured goods from developing countries predate the Treaty of Rome of 1957, these requests intensified when the Association took shape because many developing countries did not share in the benefits given by the Community to the associates. Thus the impact of the Association System has been to accelerate the global acceptance of the GSP.

The purpose of this chapter is to trace the origin and development of generalized preferences and the part played by the Association System, to discuss the advantages and disadvantages of the GSP and the GATT position in this matter, and, finally, to outline problems of implementation.

ORIGIN AND DEVELOPMENT OF GENERALIZED PREFERENCES

The first attempt to include a system of preferences in a legal code of international trade occurred in 1947 during the negotiations of the ill-fated International Trade Organization (ITO). In the Havana Charter, which was meant to lay down a set of rules for trade between nations, Article XV reads:

> The Members recognise that special circumstances, including the need for economic development or reconstruction, may justify new preferential agreements between two or more countries in the interest of the programmes of economic development or reconstruction of one or more of them.

There followed certain well-defined conditions and safeguards. Although Article XV of the Charter was seeking the acceptance of new preferential agreements for some countries, Articles XVI and XVII tried to establish a general most-favored-nation treatment and an elimination of preferences. However, the Havana Charter was not ratified and the ITO was abandoned. We have seen that the GATT accepted existing preferences but disallowed new preferences.

In the years following the signing of the GATT in 1947, the gap between developed and developing countries became a matter of concern for all, and ways and means of reducing this gap were sought. Thus, as the industrialized parts of the world began to accept the responsibility of helping the Third World, the concept of generalized preferences gained ground.

Additional support was given by special preferential arrangements entered into by certain countries, such as the 1948 agreement between the United States and some Pacific islands, between Italy and Libya in 1951 and between Australia and Papua-New Guinea in 1953.* These agreements could have paved the way for a more flexible approach to the problem of preferences for developing countries, but GATT was still wary of an extension of new preferences, and it rejected the 1954 proposal from Britain to allow preferential agreements between any developed country and a dependent territory, as well as the suggestion from Chile, in the same year, to include Article XV of the Havana Charter in the General Agreement. The reason put forward for this refusal was once again the predominance of the principle of nondiscrimination. Moreover, it was feared that this move would make certain developing countries permanently dependent on preferential treatment from their metropolis, and that the interests of those nations not included in such agreements would be impaired.

Following the signing of the Treaty of Rome in 1957, it became evident that a large number of developing countries would benefit from the newly established EEC Association System. This spurred other developing countries, especially in Latin America, to renew their pressure for a revision of the GATT rules and for special treatment of their exports. A report of a GATT Committee in 1959 concluded:

> The Committee noted that some less-developed countries have the investment and the technological resources for the processing of raw materials and are able to produce efficiently some manufactured goods. The Committee recommends that Contracting Parties, particularly industrialized countries, should urgently consider lowering barriers to the development of the export of such goods and should in their economic policies take into account the urgent need of less-developed countries to increase their export earnings and

---

*See Chapter 6.

should so far as possible avoid hindrance to the import of such goods from such countries.[1]

In 1962, this was followed by a Programme of Action proposed by less-developed countries at the Twentieth Session of the GATT. Inter alia, the following suggestions were made:

(a) Duty-free entry into the industralized countries shall be granted to tropical products by 31st December 1963;
(b) industrialized countries shall agree to the elimination of customs tariffs on the primary products important in the trade of less-developed countries;
(c) industrialized countries should also prepare urgently a schedule for the reduction and elimination of tariff barriers to exports or semi-processed and processed products from less-developed countries providing for a reduction of at least 50 per cent of the present duties over the next three years.[2]

A GATT Working Party was set up to study the problem of preferences, and the United Nations Secretariat was also asked to make a study of the matter for the Conference on Trade and Development, due to take place in 1964. During this preparation, conflicting interests emerged both among developed and developing countries. This aspect will be examined later.

The Brasseur Plan

A step toward the GSP was taken in May 1963, when M. Brasseur, the Belgian Minister of Foreign Trade and Technical Assistance, proposed a plan for generalized preferences at the GATT Ministerial Meeting of May 1963. It was a system of selective, temporary, and degressive preferences, which in fact form the basis of the GSP recently implemented by the EEC. It was hoped that most developed countries would take part, but it was not essential for all countries to do so. In the Brasseur plan, as it became known, the developed countries would not expect reciprocity for preferences granted. Efficiency of production and sales methods in developing countries would be stimulated by the fact that preferences would be temporary and degressive, and would be discontinued when the infant industries entered the competitive stage. The preferences would also be selective for three reasons: no government, accountable to the public, could undertake to give automatic preferences to all developing countries, for all manufactured goods; special care could be taken, with selective preferences, of the needs of the least-developed countries; and the

selective approach constituted a safeguard against competition of goods produced under so-called abnormal conditions, such as cheap labor, and so forth.
The GSP would be the result of negotiations initiated by developing countries.

The Brasseur plan was acceptable to the EEC since it allowed the maintenance of existing preferences to associates, but it was not formally approved
by the Six at that time because of divergence of opinion; for example, although
France supported the selective approach, Germany preferred a general system
of preferences. Several other countries, among both developed and developing
countries, disliked the idea of selective preferences.

United Nations Conference on Trade and Development (UNCTAD), 1964

The first Conference for Trade and Development, held under the auspices
of the United Nations in New York, was a disappointment for the protagonists
of GSP. Generalized preferences were discussed at length and the principle of
GSP was accepted by 69 in favor, with 8 against and 23 abstentions. Unfortunately, the United States voted against it, and no developed country would
proceed without American support. The other votes against generalized preferences were cast by Switzerland, Sweden, Canada, Finland, Iceland, Norway,
and Poland, some because they upheld the principle of nondiscrimination,
others for reasons unrelated to the scheme. The abstentions were mainly due
to the vagueness of the proposals, whereas the Soviet countries abstained
because of references to countries with "centrally planned economies."[3]

Nevertheless, in the Final Act of the Conference, the great majority of
countries agreed with the principle of "assisting the industrial development of
developing countries by the extension of preferences in their favour" and asked
the United Nations Secretary-General to arrange for a committee of government representatives to consider the matter "with a view to working out the
best method of implementing such preferences on the basis of non-reciprocity
from the developing countries."

Although the 1964 United Nations Conference on Trade and Development did not achieve a great deal from the point of view of the GSP, it helped
the developing world in other ways.

It was the first time that developing countries spoke with a collective
voice, and soon after the conference, UNCTAD was established as a permanent organ of the United Nations under the General Assembly resolution 1995
(XIX) on December 30, 1964. The resolution defined the principal functions
and membership of the Conference and its permanent organ, the Trade and
Development Board. On the recommendation of the Board, the General Assembly decided on December 20, 1965, to establish the headquarters of the
secretariat in Geneva and a liaison office at the United Nations in New York.

At its first session, the Board laid down the terms of reference of four committees: on Commodities, Manufactures, Invisibles and Financing related to trade, and Shipping. These committees meet each year and have created a number of subsidiary bodies to deal with particular problems coming under their terms of reference. "The main impact of UNCTAD comes from its recommendations which emanate mainly from developing countries and which, in general, crystallize issues they wish to have resolved so as to promote their economic and social advancement."[4]

The General Agreement on Tariffs and Trade

During the early sixties the GATT members were considering the special problems of developing countries, and the ways in which their trade could expand. It was realized that not only should the developing nations receive better prices for their primary products, but every effort should be made to encourage the production and export of semimanufactured and manufactured goods. Thus, two changes were sought in the rules of the GATT: reciprocity in tariff concessions should not be expected from developing countries; and tariff preferences should be granted to exports from developing countries, and not extended to all members of the GATT on a most-favored-nation basis.

In November 1964, the contracting parties to the GATT in their Second Special Session approved—for submission to their governments—the text of a new Part IV to the General Agreement, containing special provisions to help the trade and development of the less-developed countries. The Final Act was signed on February 8, 1965, and indicated an important change in the GATT toward the acceptance of special treatment of less-developed countries.

However, tariff concessions given by developed countries were still to follow the most-favored-nation principle and extend to all other members of the GATT, and it is this rule that became the target of attacks from developing countries. They felt that a tariff concession offered to all members of the GATT would work to the disadvantage of the less-developed countries, which would be unable to compete against more advanced producers. Thus demands became more insistent for a GSP.

The existence of two large areas of preferences, the Commonwealth and the EEC Association System, influenced the development of a GSP in two ways: on the one hand, it spurred those developing countries that did not benefit from such a system, such as the Latin American countries, to press for a system of preferences from which they would benefit; on the other hand, those countries that benefited from the existing preferential schemes were far more hesitant about a GSP that would reduce the advantages they received from their membership of the Commonwealth or their associate status.

Punta del Este

After the United Nations Conference on Trade and Development of 1964, Latin America began to press the United States for preferential treatment of their industrial goods. The United States had voted against the GSP at the Conference, but their position was weakened in 1965 by the preferential agreement with Canada for automotive products.* The first sign of a change in the U.S. attitude was the president's speech in Punta del Este, Uruguay, in 1967, where he said that his administration was prepared to explore the possibility of a GSP. This renewed interest in the scheme, and the Special Group on Trade with Developing Countries of the Organization for Economic Cooperation and Development (OECD)—led by France, the United Kingdom, Germany, and the United States—presented a report to the second session of UNCTAD in New Delhi in 1968. This proposal took the form of a summary of points that member countries of the OECD agreed should be featured in any GSP, but details were not given. Moreover, UNCTAD set up a Special Committee on Preferences.

Second UNCTAD, 1968

The problem of a GSP was discussed at the New Delhi conference, but no agreement was reached because it was found impossible to set up a single generalized preference scheme, and it was left to the developed countries to submit their own individual schemes. Moreover, most developed countries made it a condition of implementation of their scheme that all developed countries would do the same. One important drawback was that the United States threatened to abandon their scheme if discriminatory and reverse preferences were not removed from other schemes.[5]

The GATT Waiver

The introduction of generalized preferences was finally accepted and sanctioned by the GATT in 1971, in the form of a ten-year waiver, under the terms of Article XXV of the General Agreement. This allows developed countries to lower tariffs on imports from developing countries without having to extend this to all members of the GATT on a most-favored-nation basis. The waiver was requested by a number of industrialized nations, and adopted by the GATT member governments in a postal ballot.[6]

---

*See Chapter 6.

THE CASE FOR AND AGAINST GENERALIZED PREFERENCES

During the twenty-year period leading to the approval of a GSP, many arguments for and against the scheme were put forward.[7] Self-interest led some countries to stress some aspects and neglect others. We shall consider the arguments in favor and those against the GSP before examining briefly the problem of the GATT rules in this matter.

Arguments in Favor of the GSP

The most important argument for the GSP is that developing countries need help to further their economic development. In the last few years, this point has gained emphasis from the fact that the latest rounds of the GATT negotiations have not achieved a great deal for the specific problems of developing countries. Since their economy is far less advanced than the economy of industrialized nations, they need extra concessions.

Underlying this argument is the assumption that the GSP will automatically help export industries in developing countries and therefore assist in their economic development. This is similar to the well-known argument for infant industry. Newly established industries need protection in the early stages because costs per unit are high until the level of output reduces prices to competitive levels. In the same way, industries in developing countries need help, not only because most of them are in the infant stage but also because of existing conditions in developing countries in general. In those areas, the level of education and training is very low and the infrastructure of the economy is poor or nonexistent. Roads, railways, and other services have to be established and the new industries usually have to share in these costs. An additional burden is the lack of experience of both entrepreneurs and workers. If it is accepted that infant industries need help in developed areas, they certainly need greater assistance in developing countries. The question remains, however, as to whether tariff preferences are an effective way of helping.

The point has been made that two conditions must exist if tariff preferences are to help developing countries to export semimanufactured and manufactured goods.[8] First, the prices charged by the developing country must be below those of the domestic producers in the developed country giving preferences (the "donor" country), and second, the price must also be less than the price of competing goods produced in other developed countries plus the tariff applicable in each case.[9] In other words, the price of developing countries' exports may exceed those of exports from other areas, but by an amount smaller than the tariff applicable to those goods, assuming no tariff on exports from developing countries. Where the preference given is merely a lower tariff, this raises the price of developing countries' exports by the same amount.

An absence of tariffs for exports from developing countries will place these goods on an equal footing with domestic firms in the developed country, thus giving them a better chance to increase their export earnings. Again, where the preference given by the developed country is not a zero tariff, but simply a lower tariff, the prices of those exports will have to be below prices of domestic goods by the amount of the tariff.*

Other arguments put forward in favor of generalized preferences can be mentioned briefly. It has been felt for some time that foreign aid given to developing areas is not sufficient for their development and should be supplemented by easier access to the markets of developed countries. Besides, tariff preferences are more acceptable than direct aid, both from the political and psychological viewpoint. The administrative costs of such schemes to "donor" countries would be negligible and by allowing each developed country to propose their own scheme, danger of damage to their economy would be reduced to a minimum.

Arguments against the GSP

We have seen that it took a long time for countries to accept the principle of generalized preferences. The reasons for this reluctance are numerous. Some developed nations, particularly the United States, wanted to maintain the principle of nondiscrimination in tariff matters. Developing countries that benefited from special treatment were also unwilling to encourage the adoption of a GSP which would inevitably reduce their margin of preference. Regarding the GSP from a global viewpoint, the following arguments were put forward.

The most serious drawback of generalized preferences is that this will reduce the chances of further liberalization of trade, since any further tariff reduction will tend to reduce the margin of preference granted to developing countries. It is true that the GSP may be used as an excuse to maintain tariffs at their present level but this argument carries less weight if the principle of degressive preferences is accepted. Degressive preferences mean that the margin of preference will be gradually decreased. In other words, the preferential tariffs will be gradually increased until they reach the level of the normal tariff. The rate of increase will depend on each GSP proposal.

The GSP may perpetuate the economic dependence of poor countries on rich countries. This argument may be used against any form of aid to develop-

---

*The term "domestic goods" includes goods from countries that may be linked in a free-trade area or a customs union with that particular country and therefore economic integration between developed countries tends to reduce the benefits of preferences.

ing areas and it is a weak one. It must be accepted that developing countries will remain dependent on developed areas for a long time and the establishment of the GSP will not alter that situation. Moreover, it should be left to the developing countries themselves to decide on this matter, and those that dislike dependence on rich countries may elect to remain out of the scheme.

It is also maintained that the GSP may perpetuate inefficiency in the industries of developing countries. This point is often stressed in discussions on infant industry protection. It is exact that new industries tend to rely on protective tariffs once they have been granted, but it is generally accepted that it is reasonable to extend these protective tariffs to genuine cases of infant industry, in order to assist them during the early stages of growth. In the same way, the GSP is meant to help new manufacturing or processing industries in developing areas during their initial stages of growth.

Another argument against the GSP is the danger of discrimination against developing as well as developed countries. When it became evident that a single scheme could not be accepted by all countries, the fear was expressed that certain individual schemes could be arranged in such a way as to benefit some developing countries to the detriment of others, for instance, by giving better treatment to a product originating principally from a specific developing country. This is a valid argument and cannot be ignored. From the point of view of developed countries, the GSP may lead to an inequitable distribution of the burden of preferences, some developed countries "paying" more than others. It is obviously difficult if not impossible to devise a GSP that lays an equal burden on all donor countries, but as each developed country will plan and implement its own scheme, this problem is alleviated to a certain extent. It may be added that any group scheme, such as United Nations action programs or EEC common policies, falls more heavily on some countries than others and may be regarded as discriminatory by some, but this is no reason to reject international economic cooperation.

Generalized Preferences and the GATT

A consideration of the GSP in the framework of international trade should examine whether the acceptance of generalized preferences indicates a movement toward trade liberalization or another departure from the GATT principle of nondiscrimination.

It was shown above that the GSP was unacceptable for many years by members of the GATT because it discriminates against developed countries. It is only under pressure from developing countries that it was legalized by the GATT through the granting of a waiver. From the point of view of the Third World, the GSP is a means of liberalizing their trade with developed areas. If preferences succeed in increasing this trade, the conclusion can be drawn that although a discriminatory measure, the GSP is at the same time a step toward trade liberalization.

It is difficult to assess, however, whether the GSP will result in trade-creation rather than trade-diversion. If the developed countries' demand for those manufactured goods that can be produced by developing countries—and are subject to the GSP—is elastic, then it is possible that exports from developing countries may expand and benefit those areas. If on the other hand, demand is inelastic, the GSP may cause trade-diversion at the expense of the producers in other developed countries. It may therefore benefit less-efficient producers at the expense of more efficient producers, and for this reason attract criticism. On the other hand, it can be regarded as a form of aid since it involves a transfer of income from one group (in developed areas) to another (in developing areas).

As the GSP is to be established by lowering tariffs for some goods and not by raising them against others, these schemes may be regarded as being in the spirit of the GATT, in the same way as free-trade areas and customs unions, which—according to Article XXIV of the GATT—must have as their aim an increase in trade among the parties concerned and not the erection of barriers to the trade of other nations. Discrimination in international trade and trade liberalization are not necessarily mutually exclusive.

IMPLEMENTATION OF GENERALIZED PREFERENCES

Once the principle of generalized preferences for manufactured and semimanufactured goods from developing countries was accepted by most trading nations, a host of problems became apparent as details of the schemes had to be worked out.

The number of donors and of recipients was the first concern. Obviously, the ideal situation would be for all developed countries to grant preferences to all developing countries, but there could be no question of coercion. Other problems to be solved were the types of goods that should receive preferences, the depth of tariff concessions to be made, the duration of the schemes, and other provisions, such as those concerning "sensitive" products.

As regards recipients, the principle accepted was that of "self-election," whereby any country considering itself developing and eligible for GSP would apply for preferences. It was impossible to divide all trading nations into developed and developing groups as many of them are on the border line of development, but it was assumed that most of the Group of 77 would ask for preferential treatment. By the device of safeguard clauses, developed countries retain the right to refuse preferences to any developing country for particular reasons, in spite of the discriminatory aspect of such exclusions. For instance, the United States excludes countries that grant preferential treatment to products of a developed country, other than the United States, unless they have undertaken to cease doing so by 1976.[10] This clause was aimed at the EEC associates and was one of the reasons for the elimination of reverse preferences in the Lomé Convention.

It was hoped at some stage that the least advanced among developing nations could receive special treatment in a GSP, although the earlier plans were to have a completely nondiscriminatory system. The first point obviously contradicts the second. Nevertheless, the hope was expressed that "special preferences could be granted to the less advanced developing countries" and at the same time, "the ultimate objective should be to adapt existing preferential arrangements to the new system of preferences in such a way that there is no discrimination among developing countries, and so that developing countries presently obtaining such preferences should continue receiving benefits under the new system at least equivalent to those they now enjoy."[11] The term "equivalent" is ambiguous, as those countries enjoying preferences prior to the establishment of GSP may stand to lose if all developing countries are granted preferences in the same markets. It must be accepted that either the GSP is nondiscriminatory, that is, applied equally to all developing countries, or exceptions are made for the least-developed areas, and for those who were receiving special treatment before the establishment of the GSP.

Although some developing countries regarded the GSP as a threat to their own trade, since it would automatically reduce the margin of preference given to their goods in certain markets, such as the EEC or the Commonwealth, they finally accepted the GSP because they hoped that what would be lost in "traditional" markets would be gained by preferential entry into new markets.

Developing countries that had not previously received preferential treatment welcomed the general acceptance of GSP but some of them felt that the number of goods covered and the depth of the tariff cuts were insufficient. These points were raised at an UNCTAD meeting in 1970, and a speaker for the EEC replied that the proposals were the result of "enormous effort and that it was the maximum possible at this stage."[12]

From the point of view of the donor countries, the drawbacks of the GSP include administrative costs and increased competition for domestic goods as well as competition in other developed countries' markets. Certain aspects of the scheme, as for example the selection of the goods to benefit from preferences, may cause a certain amount of political friction among both donors and recipients.

Attitudes of developed countries vary: the EEC and the United Kingdom regard the GSP as an extension of their present system of preferences to some developing countries, while the United States considers preferences as a deviation from their normal policy of nondiscrimination and thus have only recently and somewhat reluctantly accepted the principle of the GSP.

It was finally accepted that no agreement would be reached on a single scheme of preferences and that the best way to proceed was to leave each donor country to propose and implement its own scheme.

Since the GATT waiver of 1971, several developed countries grant generalized preferences to manufactured goods from developing countries.

> Preferential schemes under the GSP have been implemented by the European Economic Community, Japan, Norway, Denmark, Finland, Ireland, New Zealand, Sweden, the United Kingdom, Switzerland and Austria. Two countries, the United States and Canada, have not yet put into effect their schemes of generalized preferences. Australia has been granting tariff preferences to developing countries since 1966.
>
> Of the socialist countries of Eastern Europe, Bulgaria, Czechoslovakia and Hungary have introduced preferential schemes of generalized preferences. The USSR has provided duty-free entry for imports of goods from developing countries since 1965.[13]

Several schemes are implemented on the principle of selective preferences, that is, a selection of manufactured and semimanufactured goods receive preferential treatment. Most GSP have been established for a period of ten years and all of them (except Japan's) incorporate an escape clause "which allows the preferences to be modified in the event of a claim of injury to domestic producers or proven disruption of markets."[14] In addition, the EEC scheme offers preferences only up to a certain ceiling, and the EEC, Britain, and the United States exclude most textiles from their schemes.

Although the United Kingdom scheme was more advantageous than the EEC's, since it offered preferences without ceilings, the enlargement of the Community will require the harmonization of the GSP of the EEC, Britain, Ireland, and Denmark.

Generalized preferences are among the topics discussed at the GATT round proceeding in Geneva at present (the "Tokyo round") and there is evidence of conflicting interests between developed and developing countries. Since any tariff reduction agreed upon by developed countries between themselves will lower the preference margin given through the GSP, developing countries are asking for a binding of these margins. This would mean, for instance, that if a most-favored-nation (MFN) duty is 15 percent and the GSP rate 10 percent, a reduction of the MFN duty to say, 8 percent would force the preference-giving country concerned to bring the GSP rate down to 3 percent. Developed countries, on the other hand, fear that a binding of preference margins would hamper efforts to reduce tariffs generally and they also dislike the inflexibility that this would bring to the GSP.[15]

ASSESSMENT

After some twenty years of pressure for and discussions about the GSP, it was generally accepted for two main reasons. The purpose of the scheme is the economic development of the Third World and it is regarded as nondiscriminatory because it is meant to apply to all developing countries. The second point explains why the GSP has not attracted the same criticism as the EEC Association System, in spite of the fact that, in practice, the GSP involves some discrimination, even among developing countries.

If we compare the GSP and economic integration, they both contain elements of free trade and discrimination, but they differ in two important aspects: GSP tariff concessions are not reciprocal, as were the EEC concessions under the Yaounde Convention; and GSP concessions are partial since they apply only to manufactured and semimanufactured products from developing countries.

Every effort should be made to bridge the gap between the rich and poor countries, but it is doubtful whether generalized preferences will aid industrialization of developing areas. We have seen that free entry into the European Community has not had a great effect upon the trade results of associated countries and it will probably be the same for the GSP. Moreover, industrial tariffs being generally low, preferential rates applied to exports from developing countries will have a minimal effect on their economy. Problems of development are considerable and cannot be solved by a few tariff concessions.

On the other hand, as generalized preferences are urgently requested by developing countries, implementation of this scheme by a large number of developed nations may have a salutary psychological effect on the relationship between the poor and rich countries, and should therefore be carried out. It can be added that the chances of effectiveness of the GSP might be increased if the terms of the schemes were more generous—for instance, applying zero tariffs to textile exports from developing areas—but developed countries are not prepared to go this far. It must also be remembered that the GSP is barely five years old and that a longer period of time is needed to assess more accurately its possible effects on developing countries.[16]

From the global point of view, the GSP discriminates against developed countries and is an important departure from the principle of nondiscrimination. However, the GSP is not the only deviation from the GATT rule of equality of treatment in trade matters. The following chapter will consider several other factors that have contributed to the failure of the principle of nondiscrimination.

NOTES

1. General Agreement on Tariffs and Trade, *Basic Instruments and Selected Documents, Eighth Supplement,* Geneva, 1960, p. 140.

2. General Agreement on Tariffs and Trade, *Basic Instruments and Selected Documents, Eleventh Supplement,* Geneva, 1963, pp. 205–06.

3. In February 1965 the Soviet Union informed the United Nations that it had abolished customs duties on all goods imported from the less-developed countries. New York *Times,* February 5, 1965, p. 39.

4. Edgar Jones, "The Fund and UNCTAD," *Finance and Development* 8, no. 3 (September 1971): 29.

5. See David Wall, "EEC General Preferences: How Effective Will They Be?" *European Community,* January 1972, p. 22.

6. The GATT Press Release 1082, June 26, 1971.

7. See inter alia, John Pincus, *Trade, Aid and Development* (New York: McGraw-Hill, 1967), pp. 197 ff.

8. Gardner Patterson, "Would Tariff Preferences Help Economic Development?" *Lloyds Bank Review,* no. 76 (April 1965), p. 25.

9. Whether "nominal" or "effective" tariff. For discussion on this point see H. G. Johnson, "Trade Preferences and Developing Countries," *Lloyds Bank Review,* no. 80 (April 1966), pp. 13ff. See also John Pincus, *Trade, Aid and Development,* pp. 189–90.

10. See Jean Royer, "The United States Trade Reform Bill: Background Note," International Chamber of Commerce, Document 102/106, Paris, 1973. Economic and Financial Policy, Commission on the Expansion of International Trade, p. 10. See also GATT, Generalized Preferences, Notification by the United States, L/4299, February 13, 1976, p. 3.

11. Raúl Prebisch, "Towards a New Trade Policy for Development," in *Reshaping the World Economy: Rich Countries and Poor,* ed. John A. Pincus (Englewood Cliffs, N.J.: Prentice-Hall, 1968), p. 122.

12. UNCTAD Press Release, TAD/INF/459(PREF), September 23, 1970.

13. UNCTAD Monthly Bulletin no. 80, April 1973.

14. Wall, "EEC General Preferences: How Effective Will They Be?" p. 22.

15. See S. J. Anjaria, "The Multinational Trade Negotiations and Tariff Reduction," *Finance and Development* 12, no. 4 (December 1975): 28.

16. See T. Murray, "How Helpful Is the Generalized System of Preferences to Developing Countries?" *The Economic Journal* 83, no. 330 (June 1973): 449–55.

CHAPTER

8

FAILURE OF THE GATT'S RULE OF NONDISCRIMINATION

When the General Agreement on Tariffs and Trade was signed in 1947, the contracting parties agreed to two main principles. The first was that member countries should grant each other the same favorable treatment in trade matters as they grant any other member country. This is commonly called the most-favored-nation clause and has long been a feature of commercial treaties; in the context of the GATT it is usually described as the principle of nondiscrimination. The second principle is that protection should be given only by means of tariffs and that these should be progressively reduced in order to liberalize international trade.

A consideration of the achievements of the GATT over the last 25 years leads to the conclusion that the principle of nondiscrimination has been a failure, whereas the principle of tariff reduction has been successfully applied. The purpose of this chapter is to draw attention to the causes of the failure of the first principle of the GATT, and the part played by the Association System of the EEC.

Several factors have weakened the principle of nondiscrimination but the fundamental cause of this failure lies in the unrealistic expectation of equality of treatment on a worldwide scale, as was envisaged by the founders of the GATT. Trade interests have forced certain countries to enter into discriminatory arrangements with others, and this was made possible by the early acceptance of exceptions to the rule, which vitiated the principle of nondiscrimination from the beginning.

CONTRIBUTORY FACTORS

The factors that contributed to the failure of the most-favored-nation principle are as follows:

1. Article I excludes a number of established preferences of long standing from the most-favored-nation principle.

2. Article XXIV allows customs unions, free-trade areas, and interim arrangements, opening the way to "legal" discrimination.

3. Article XIV permits the discriminatory application of quantitative import restrictions to protect the balance of payments in special circumstances.

4. Article XXXV permits the nonapplication of the GATT rules between certain contracting parties.

5. Part IV of the GATT, introduced in 1965, exempts developing countries from several of the GATT rules.

6. The recently established Generalized System of Preferences allows discrimination in favor of developing countries in the application of tariffs for manufactured and semimanufactured goods.

7. Finally, the GATT is unable to prevent an increasing number of preferential arrangements that do not quite conform to the rules laid down in the General Agreement.

Article I

The first article of the GATT illustrates the compromise between those contracting parties that upheld nondiscrimination as the main rule, and those who were not prepared to give up their existing system of preferences. (This point has been discussed in Chapter 6.) Thus, the GATT insisted that the most-favored-nation treatment should be applied between members, but allowed existing preferences to remain, such as those applied in the British Commonwealth, the French Union, and others. It was obviously a weakness to draw a distinction between existing preferences and new preferences, and consequently several new preferences have been accepted by the GATT members, either by the grant of a waiver or tacitly. Although it was first hoped that existing preferences would be progressively abolished, the practical outcome was that the margin of preference would not be increased. Thus, Article I introduced a weakness into the main GATT rule from the beginning.

Article XXIV

This article specifically allows free-trade areas, customs unions, and interim agreements leading to the formation of either kind of economic integration, provided that certain conditions are met: first, the tariffs of the customs union must not be higher than those of the member countries prior to union, and second, the arrangements must involve "substantially all the trade" between the parties. This article has been invoked several times since the signing of the GATT, due to the growth of regional integration. From the point of view of international trade, customs unions and free-trade areas illustrate the duality of nondiscrimination within the customs union, and discrimination toward nonmembers. This makes it difficult to decide whether regional integration is a step toward trade liberalization or a step away from it. If this trend is regarded as the creation of larger customs territories, then the abolition of tariff barriers between the countries forming the customs union indicates a liberalization of trade, even if this is not extended to all contracting parties of the GATT, in other words, even if it is discriminatory. Furthermore, the loose wording of Article XXIV has led to a wide interpretation of the expression "interim agreements" and "substantially all the trade," as shown in the EEC Association and trade agreements and in the Stockholm Convention of 1960, establishing the European Free Trade Association. Thus certain agreements are regarded by some as conforming to Article XXIV of the GATT, and by others as preferential agreements (see Chapter 6).

Article XIV

Exceptions to the rule of nondiscrimination, as regards quantitative restrictions, are contained in Article XIV. Although these restrictions are generally forbidden by the GATT, they are allowed in cases of balance-of-payments difficulties, as long as they are applied nondiscriminately (Article XIII). However, Article XIV contains provisions that authorize the discriminatory application of quantitative restrictions in special cases. Several contracting parties have evoked this article in support of their import control policies, among them the Republic of South Africa.

Article XXXV

The General Agreement includes other "escape clauses" such as Article XXXV, which gives any contracting party the possibility of not applying the GATT rules to another party. This was the last article of the original agreement. The nonapplication may occur if the two parties have not entered into tariff negotiations with each other, and if either party, at the time one of them becomes a member of the GATT, does not consent to such application.

This article has been invoked by South Africa against Japan, and by India against South Africa, the first for economic reasons, and the second for political reasons. It has also been invoked in other cases, but the most striking example was that concerning the accession of Japan to the GATT. When this country finally became a contracting party in 1955—its membership had been deferred for many years for a variety of reasons—fourteen countries representing about 40 percent of the foreign trade of the GATT's members invoked Article XXXV against Japan. This article has been called "the great loophole" because it opened the door to widespread discriminatory practices for protective purposes.[1]

The factors mentioned so far were all part of the General Agreement when it was signed in 1947. They indicate the unwillingness of the contracting parties to commit themselves unconditionally to the principle of nondiscrimination. This led to the inclusion of these exceptions that covered most likely problems, but on the other hand, these exceptions vitiate the main principle to a considerable extent and may be construed as an example of bad faith on the part of the original signatories. The principle of equality of treatment was upheld as the main principle of the GATT, but provision was made for ways to avoid it when trade interests are in danger. However, several countries might have refused to participate in the GATT if these escape clauses had been absent.

Part IV of the GATT

In 1965, a new chapter was added to the General Agreement to deal with the special problems of developing countries, although Article XVIII dealt with the conditions under which countries may deviate from the rules of the GATT in order to encourage their economic development. The new section, Articles XXXVI to XXXVIII, deals with such exceptions in greater detail, and lays down the commitments of developed countries in this respect. The most explicit departure from the principle of nondiscrimination is Section 8 of Article XXXVI by which developed contracting parties do not expect reciprocity from developing countries in trade matters. The new chapter aims at assisting the trade of developing countries, but it also stresses disparities between developed and developing areas.

Generalized Preferences

The establishment of a Generalized System of Preferences for manufactured goods from developing countries is legalized under the GATT, by the granting of a waiver from the rule of nondiscrimination to the developed countries who request it. This is a major deviation from the first principle of the GATT, as was shown in Chapter 7, especially since the GSP is not equally applied to all developing countries and individual schemes lead to a variety of treatment of goods and countries.

The previous two paragraphs concern developing countries. These deviations from the main principle of the GATT are explained by the fact that although the original agreement was signed by only 23 countries in 1947, many nations acquired independence during the following years, and by 1965, a large number of the new contracting parties were developing nations and differed in many ways from the original signatories to the General Agreement. It soon became evident that the rules framed for developed countries were inadequate for the needs of developing countries, and therefore, further exceptions were made to the principle of nondiscrimination.

Preferential Agreements

We have seen that several preferential agreements were condoned by the GATT through the granting of waivers. (See Chapter 6.) In addition, even though some of the agreements of the EEC Association System do not quite conform to the rules of the GATT, divided opinions have increased the possibility of a de facto acceptance of these agreements, especially where they concern developing countries. Finally, the recent formation of the European free-trade zone of 16 nations illustrates yet another contravention of the GATT's Article I. As these EEC-EFTA arrangements concern developed countries and have aroused criticism from the United States, it is worthwhile considering these agreements in some detail.

The European Free Trade Association was formed in 1960 by seven countries when Great Britain, Portugal, Austria, Switzerland, and the three Scandinavian countries signed the Stockholm Convention. The later accession of Finland and Iceland brought the total to nine. In 1972, the entry of two EFTA members, Britain and Denmark, into the European Community necessitated new arrangements between the remaining seven members of EFTA and the enlarged EEC, in order to prevent new trade barriers from arising between Britain and Denmark, on the one hand, and EFTA countries on the other.

The Stockholm Convention did not include trade in agricultural goods and therefore, it may be said that the free-trade area of EFTA did not include "substantially all the trade," as laid down by Article XXIV of the GATT. However, EFTA did not receive a waiver to legalize this exception. Instead, a working party of the GATT examined the terms of the Convention and reported on it, concluding that "there remain some legal and practical issues which would not be fruitfully discussed further at this stage. Accordingly, the contracting parties do not find it appropriate to make recommendations to the parties. . . ."[2] Thus, although the GATT found that the Stockholm Convention did not quite conform to the provisions of Article XXIV, it was considered not important enough to make recommendations and demand modifications.

The agreements between the EEC and EFTA countries also exclude agricultural products, and it is reasonable to assume that the same attitude will prevail in the GATT. As the EFTA members have no common external tariff, seven separate agreements were negotiated with the EEC.

It is interesting to note that some EFTA members such as Switzerland and Sweden, which were outspoken supporters of the principle of nondiscrimination and critical of preferential arrangements, urged the EEC to come to terms with EFTA and to abolish tariffs between them. It appears that most nations do not disapprove of discrimination as a matter of principle, but object when discrimination threatens their own interests.

> The Scandinavians, who had led the critics of the Coal and Steel Community, apparently raised but few objections to the EEC proposals. From the outset, they thought they would sooner or later get inside the preferential walls, first as part of the original European-wide area scheme, and, later, in the melding of the European Free Trade Association with the Common Market.[3]

It should be mentioned here, that a wide free-trade zone in Europe is not a new idea. In 1955, Britain, who did not want to commit herself to the closer integration planned by the Six, suggested the formation of a free-trade area among the countries belonging to the OEEC.[4] This was rejected by the Six, but when the Common Market showed signs of success, the idea of linking the EEC with EFTA was promoted once again and has now become a reality.

EVALUATION

The above discussion brings us to the conclusion that the principle of nondiscrimination of the GATT has been a failure, since it is evident that discrimination in international trade cannot be eliminated. The numerous exceptions to Article I have weakened the main principle of the General Agreement and in addition, subsequent developments, such as the GSP and the Association System have all contributed to the ineffectiveness of the main principle of the GATT.

The underlying cause of this failure lies in the difference between the contracting parties of the GATT. Not only are there wide differences in their level of economic development, but also in the pattern and evolution of their external trade. Differences in economic development account for recent changes in the GATT rules, such as the GSP, while differences in trade patterns have led to regional arrangements of various forms, such as free-trade areas and customs unions, with their inherent discrimination against nonmembers. It is understandable that this trend is viewed with alarm by those who regard equality in international trade as essential.

Disparities between countries and between trade patterns lead to differences in outlook and objectives. Some look for economic development, others for self-efficiency, others still for a global efficiency in international trade. Thus their aims differ, and their policies follow. Consequently, countries consider discrimination differently. Some see it as a real and dangerous barrier to international trade, while others consider discriminatory measures as necessary to promote their own external trade.

These differences of opinion explain the continuing tensions in multilateral trade negotiations, such as the current GATT talks. The next chapter shall examine in more detail these sources of conflict in international trade.

NOTES

1. See Gardner Patterson, *Discrimination in International Trade, The Policy Issues* (Princeton: Princeton University Press, 1966), p. 19.

2. General Agreement on Tariffs and Trade, *Basic Instruments and Selected Documents, Ninth Supplement,* Geneva, 1961, p. 20.

3. Gardner Patterson, *Discrimination in International Trade,* p. 156, footnote 60.

4. Organization for European Economic Cooperation, which became the Organization for Economic Cooperation and Development in 1961.

9

SOURCES OF CONFLICT IN
INTERNATIONAL TRADE

In September 1973, a new round of multilateral trade negotiations was inaugurated in Tokyo, under the auspices of the GATT. The talks are proceeding in Geneva and a variety of problems will be considered, including tariff and nontariff barriers to trade in industrial and agricultural products, as well as the special needs of developing countries. Until now, discussions have centered around procedure and organization of the complex bargaining, which is likely to take several years. Ninety-three countries are participating in the Tokyo round, among which are several nonmembers of the GATT.[1]

It is probable that some GATT rules will be altered as a result of these negotiations. Pressure will be brought to bear on developed countries to improve their GSP schemes (see Chapter 7) or to help developing countries in other ways. Regional arrangements will be under attack as well as the principle of nondiscrimination. Efforts will be made to contain the increase in protectionism, which began soon after the Kennedy round of the GATT ended in 1967.

It will not be a simple task for so many nations to agree on solutions to such varied problems. The Kennedy round lasted three years and the six members of the European Community took five years to agree on the details of the common agricultural policy of the EEC. The difficulty lies not so much in the fact that time is needed to examine a large number of problems but rather in the probability that different viewpoints are bound to lead to conflict.

Constantly changing circumstances would not present such a challenge to the GATT if all the Contracting Parties shared a common view of their precise objectives. Then common policies and programs might be thrashed out. But the fact is that Contracting Parties have differing views of the function of international trade.[2]

Some countries feel that trade between nations should be carried out with a view to greater economic efficiency; others stress economic development and industrialization; yet others aim at self-sufficiency and seek to protect infant industries.

This chapter examines the causes underlying these differences that lead to conflict in international trade and are likely to handicap the search for the common interest of all trading nations.

The problem is complicated by clashes of sectoral interests within a particular nation; moreover, where negotiations take place with groups such as the EEC, a new dimension is added. Thus besides clashes between sectors of the economy and between sectors and the nation as a whole, there may be conflicts of interests between the members of the group and finally between the group and other negotiating nations. In this maze of diverse interests, negotiators have to look for the common interest without losing sight of the interest of their own nation. It is therefore understandable that sometimes they confuse the two in order to facilitate the task!

In multilateral negotiations, efforts are made toward an ideal framework of international trade, but the elements of this framework vary according to characteristics of negotiating countries. More specifically, the attitudes of nations are influenced by the stage of development of their economy, the size of their internal market, existing patterns of trade, the efficiency of their export industries, and social and political considerations, while procedures of negotiations are complicated by differences in tariff structures and other customs regulations.

An examination of each of these aspects will bring out the causes underlying conflicts in international trade.

STAGE OF DEVELOPMENT

Wide differences of opinion exist between developed and developing countries as to the aims of international trade. Developed nations tend to stress efficiency in international trade with elimination of trade barriers. Developing countries on the other hand seek mainly an improvement in their economies and especially industrialization. Concessions are requested in order to encourage exports of semimanufactured goods as well as primary products, and preferential treatment in the markets of developed countries is sought. The Third World is not impressed by the argument that international trade should be nondiscriminatory. If the GSP offers some hope of improving terms of trade for developing countries, they favor it even if it discriminates against developed countries. Where possible, some developing countries go further and enter into special arrangements, such as association or trade agreements with the EEC. If necessary they are prepared to give reverse preferences to form free-trade areas or other forms of economic integration in the hope of encouraging development.

Moreover, the issues are complicated by the fact that attitudes of developing countries toward the GSP and reverse preferences vary according to whether they have already formed close associations with developed countries or not. The former accept the principle of reverse preferences[3] while others look upon them as an "archaic and pernicious hangover from another age."[4] It has been shown that some developing countries welcome the GSP but others fear that this new scheme will reduce the preferences that they have hitherto enjoyed in the markets of some developed countries.

Although certain developed countries stress the aim of trade liberalization and nondiscrimination, many of them endeavor to see the viewpoint of the Third World. In view of the general acceptance of the needs of developing nations, exceptions have been made regarding certain GATT rules and a number of industrialized nations have offered generalized preferences to developing countries.

SIZE OF INTERNAL MARKET

The size of the internal market influences attitudes on economic integration. A country with a small internal market looks upon integration as a means of expanding the market and encouraging large-scale production and specialization. Thus a nation may decide to form a free-trade area or an economic union and to ignore arguments against this form of discrimination. On the other hand, a country with a large internal market and wide scope for large-scale production has no need for such integration and stresses the discriminatory aspects of regional integration as well as the need for equality of treatment for all trading nations. Members of the EEC, associates, and others favor free-trade areas and similar arrangements while the United States, with its large internal market, generally favors nondiscrimination on a worldwide scale. This does not mean that all countries with small internal markets wish to integrate with others. Japan, for example, has been able to expand her markets abroad and to compensate for the shortcomings of her local market. Britain on the other hand, found that worldwide trade links were no longer adequate and sought integration with the Six in order to increase the scope of her industries.

PATTERNS OF TRADE

Past and present trade patterns affect the position of trading nations on certain aspects of international trade. Countries that have for many years exported to certain markets tend to consider that they have a prior claim to those outlets, while others seek to increase exports and look forward to getting a foothold in new markets. Thus some nations prefer the status quo and others look for change. A striking example is the case of the United States and Canada, which have been described as the "traditional" or "established" exporters of farm products, especially to the EEC, and view apprehensively the increase in agricultural production caused by the common agricultural policy.[5] On the other hand, New Zealand has had to seek other markets for dairy products in view of Britain's entry into the Common Market and has recently increased exports to Asian countries, while Japan has increased sales to the United States to such a degree that she has been asked to organize "voluntary" export control for certain products.

In another context, efforts are made to alter the traditional pattern of trade whereby developed countries export manufactured goods to developing countries and import primary products from them. This trend is still apparent in the trade of some developed countries and their ex-dependencies, notably in Africa. Countries that benefit from these links are prepared to maintain them, but others—both among developed and developing countries—attack these patterns of trade as relics of the colonial era or as neocolonialism, and favor their elimination.

EFFICIENCY

The degree of efficiency of a country's industries affects multilateral trade talks. A country with several low-cost producers tends to support measures that stress efficiency in international trade and to condemn methods likely to distort free competition. Worldwide removal of barriers to multilateral trade will therefore be favored. On the other hand, countries with high-cost industries try to improve their position and protect their local industries with both tariff and nontariff barriers, disregarding arguments that the more efficient producers should provide the goods. The dividing line does not necessarily separate developed and developing countries. Among developed nations too, some are more concerned about efficiency in international trade, while others may be willing to protect a new industry or some other sector of the economy. For example, agricultural production in parts of the European Community is less efficient than in the United States, yet both maintain agricultural protectionism. There may be a variety of reasons for this: national prestige, desire for self-sufficiency, pressure groups, or other considerations.

SOCIAL AND POLITICAL FACTORS

These may also alter the bargaining position of negotiating countries. They give rise to "sensitive" areas of trade policy. Most developed countries sympathize with demands by developing countries for outlets for their growing industries but at the same time, industrialized nations are obliged to consider depressed or underdeveloped areas within their borders. Understandably, these areas have a prior claim. This is the reason for the exclusion of textiles from the GSP offer by the United States. Although it is generally accepted that the problem of underdevelopment would be helped by encouragement of labor-intensive industries such as textiles, the United States wishes to protect the textile sector of the economy from low-cost competitors, because the low-income group of her population depends on this form of employment.

Agriculture is another "sensitive" area in trade policy, and perhaps the most important one. The Kennedy round of the GATT did not achieve a great deal in this sector.

> It would be difficult to conclude that the GATT's record in the sphere of temperate agricultural commodities is other than one of failure. Not only is effective protection in all likelihood higher on average than in any other sector of the international economy, but there are many indications that the rate of effective protection is increasing.[6]

Most countries in the Western world protect agriculture and this is also the case for Japan. There is no plan to liberalize Japanese agriculture in spite of difficulties due to labor shortages and other aspects. As in the EEC, a large proportion of the farmers are elderly and the typical farm is small. Yet measures such as exposure to foreign competition, which would cause dissatisfaction among the peasants, are avoided for political reasons. During a discussion between the Japanese and American governments on trade liberalization in 1968,

> whereas Japan offered no resistance in principle to the proposals for the liberalization of several classes of industrial products, including electronic goods, they refused the American request to remove restrictions on the import of various agricultural products, including beef.[7]

In the EEC, the Common Agricultural Policy has been framed for the purpose of improving the standard of living of the farming community by protecting them from low-priced imports, improving the structure and efficiency of farms and other measures. In the same way as it is felt that the Third World needs help, so the Community is prepared to support and assist farmers that constitute a depressed sector in the Common Market. Thus social and political considerations add complexity to differences of opinion in international negotiations.

TARIFF STRUCTURES

Conflict becomes apparent in trade negotiations with regard to the methods used in reducing tariffs because nations have different tariff structures. This was evident at the beginning of the Kennedy round and is once again under discussion in the Tokyo round of the GATT. The United States, with a large number of high tariffs, is in favor of linear cuts, that is, a reduction of all tariffs by 50 percent or some other acceptable percentage, whereas the EEC supports the objective of tariff harmonization, the reduction of high tariffs to lower levels. The Common Market, with a relatively low common external tariff for industrial goods, proposed the procedure of *écrêtement* (literally, "taking the peaks off") to reduce high tariffs, but this may be rejected in favor of reciprocal linear cuts.

Nontariff barriers are also controversial and countries will no doubt attack those barriers used by others but try to preserve those that form part of their customs regulations and formalities. The GATT has compiled a catalog of some 800 nontariff barriers classified in 27 categories.[8] "Subsequently, it was agreed that the Committee should focus on a few specific nontariff barriers that appeared least controversial and thus most likely to be amenable to multilateral negotiations."[9]

Sources of conflict in international trade have been examined separately but they often overlap and this aspect complicates issues further. Moreover, nations will not necessarily find themselves on the same side for the duration of negotiations, for they may agree on some points and disagree on others.

This review of differences in attitudes, opinions, and objectives among trading nations may lead to a pessimistic view of the current GATT negotiations. Is there a "common" interest or simply a number of national and sectoral interests that are bound to clash? One may find some reassurance in the evolution of the EEC: after the failure of the European Defense Community in 1954, it may have seemed that a united Europe was doomed. Yet the Messina conference of 1955 led to the Rome Treaty two years later. Once the objective of an economic union was agreed upon, solutions were found to conflicting national interests. Difficulties will be far greater, however, in multilateral talks including a large number of nations of such diversity. The only hope lies in an increase of the international—as opposed to national—outlook, which might be assisted by some form of supranational thinking in international trade.

NOTES

1. See GATT, *Press Release*, "The 1973 Multilateral Trade Negotiations: The Crucial Choices Ahead." Address by Mr. Olivier Long, May 3, 1973. GATT/1122. Also, GATT, *Press*

Release, "GATT, the Multilateral Trade Negotiations and the Developing Countries," Address by Mr. O. Long, March 8, 1976. GATT/1176.

2. Kenneth W. Dam, *The GATT Law and International Economic Organization* (Chicago: University of Chicago Press, 1970), p. 6.

3. See Okigbo, *Africa and the Common Market* (London: Longmans, 1967), p. 130.

4. W. Michael Blumenthal, "A World of Preferences," *Foreign Affairs* 48, no. 3 (April 1970): 554.

5. Hugh Corbet, ed., *Trade Strategy and the Asian-Pacific Region* (London: Allen & Unwin, 1970), p. 21.

6. Dam, *The GATT Law,* p. 257.

7. G. C. Allen, "Japan's Place in Trade Strategy," in Corbet, *Trade Strategy and the Asian-Pacific Region,* p. 97n.

8. For example, escape clauses, antidumping practices, customs valuations, government procurement policies, state trading, mixing regulations. See H. G. Johnson, ed., *New Trade Strategy for the World Economy* (London: Allen & Unwin, ,1969), p. 36n.

9. International Monetary Fund, *IMF Survey,* August 27, 1973, p. 244.

CHAPTER
10
CONCLUSIONS

The Association System of the European Economic Community has inaugurated a new trend in international trade. The network of association and trade agreements has reduced trade barriers and given financial and technical assistance to many developing countries. It is a manifestation of the growing tendency toward economic integration and therefore, both liberate trade between some countries and discriminate against others.

The main impact of the Association has been on Africa, since thirty-seven African states have entered into agreements with the Community. The inclusion of Commonwealth countries into the Association is eroding the old division between Francophone and Anglophone Africa and is changing the attitude of many developing countries toward these arrangements.

The analysis of trade figures between the associates and the EEC showed little improvement over a period of 16 years. But it would be imprudent to conclude that the Association has had no effect on the associates as a whole.

The theory of customs unions demonstrates the effects of integration on the levels of production and consumption of member countries and the impact of this change on trade with outside countries. It fails to generalize on whether the overall effect is favorable or not, because it concentrates on only a few of the many variables in the economies concerned. The value of the more recent literature on integration is that it enlarges the field of investigation and demonstrates that the sociopolitical aspects of customs unions and economic unions are inextricably linked with the economic factors. This is why empirical studies of the effects of integration are inevitably limited to a particular sector of the communities concerned, and cannot claim to illustrate the overall effect of economic integration.

Even if detailed statistics on growth and investment in associated countries were available, it cannot be proven that changes in these fields are the result of economic integration with the EEC. The present state of theory does not allow us to isolate changes due to integration and those that are the result of other causes. The field is wide open to speculation.

There is no evidence that the Association has damaged the trade of nonassociates, and on the positive side, it has led to a diversification of the trade of associates among members of the EEC, and the enlargement of the Community from six to nine will no doubt amplify this development.

South Africa's trade with Britain will be affected by Britain's entry into the EEC but it is difficult to give an accurate estimate of this change. By the time the common external tariff is fully implemented in 1977, progress in marketing practices and export promotion on the part of South African exporters may offset the loss of preference in the British market. Although it is doubtful whether South Africa can ever become an associate of the EEC, due to her level of economic development and political factors, a trade agreement with the Community is a possibility. The South African Customs Union may have to be reexamined now that Botswana, Swaziland, and Lesotho, Commonwealth members of the union, have become associates of the EEC.

The principle of nondiscrimination of the GATT received a severe blow when most trading nations agreed to the principle of Generalized Preferences. This provides easier entry for manufactured goods from developing countries into the markets of developed areas, and thereby assists in the economic development of the Third World. The Association System of the EEC contributed to the GSP by spurring nonassociates to demand preferences similar to those given by the EEC to their associates.

In spite of Article I of the GATT stressing the need for equality in trade matters, there is evidence of substantial discrimination in international trade, partly due to the impossibility of a strict application of the principle and partly due to the growing trend toward economic integration. A revision of the GATT rules on this point is indicated and it is possible that this will be discussed at the Tokyo round. The success of these talks will depend on the recognition of the various positions that may be taken regarding the purpose of international trade and on the amount of tolerance shown toward different viewpoints.

It is generally accepted that developing countries need some form of discrimination in their favor—although some would prefer a rigid adherence to the principle of nondiscrimination—but many advocate universal arrangements such as the Generalized System of Preferences rather than regional ones. On the other hand, regional agreements have their supporters.

> Contrary to what many seem to believe, the goal of a development policy should not be complete liberalisation of trade. Only a limited number of countries would profit from such measures. That is why I am in favour of association and preferential trade agreements, as long as the picture of an underdeveloped world of identical nations is wrong.[1]

Problems of developing countries will feature prominently in the GATT discussions. The EEC is currently formulating a development policy. The Treaty of Rome does not mention the Community's position vis-a-vis developing countries because in 1957 it was primarily concerned with the establishment of an economic union in Europe, and only provided for the relationship between the Six and their dependencies. In 1972 however, the Summit Conference of the EEC called upon the member states to implement a comprehensive policy of worldwide development cooperation, without losing sight of the vital importance of the maintenance and development of the Association.[2]

The controversy that has surrounded the Association System since its inception is showing signs of abatement. Several reasons account for this. First, the extension of the Association, through the Lomé Convention, to new parts of Africa, the Caribbean, and the Pacific, illustrates the widespread acceptability of economic links with the European Community. Second, free-trade arrangements between the enlarged Community and remaining members of the European Free Trade Association have led to a more tolerant interpretation of Article XXIV of the GATT. Third, the majority of GATT members are now either members of the EEC, associates, or countries that have signed a trade agreement with the Community, and this has reduced the effectiveness of criticism of the Association as a whole. Finally, the attention of the trading nations of the world is focused less on tariff matters and more on problems such as currency and mobility of factors of production.

In the framework of international trade policy, the Association System of the EEC has an impact that extends far beyond the countries concerned. It influences the development of a Community policy toward the Third World and increases the probability of changes in the GATT rules. However, the main achievement of the Association is a contribution to trade liberalization and industrial cooperation between an ever-increasing number of countries, and the creation of a unique link between some of the richest and poorest countries of the world.

NOTES

1. R. Cohen, "Europe and the Developing Countries, Summary of the Discussions," in *The European Community in the World,* Ph. P. Everts, ed. (Rotterdam: University Press, 1972), p. 194.

2. See *Commission of the European Communities.* Memorandum of the Commission to the Council on the Future Relations between the Community, the Present AAMS States and the Countries in Africa, COM(73) 500/fin. Luxembourg, 1973.

PART FOUR: THE ASSOCIATION OF OVERSEAS COUNTRIES AND TERRITORIES

Article 131

The Member States hereby agree to bring into association with the Community the non-European countries and territories which have special relations with Belgium, France, Italy and the Netherlands. These countries and territories, hereinafter referred to as "the countries and territories," are listed in Annex IV to this Treaty.

The purpose of this association shall be to promote the economic and social development of the countries and territories and to establish close economic relations between them and the Community as a whole.

In conformity with the principles stated in the Preamble to this Treaty, this association shall in the first place permit the furthering of the interests and prosperity of the inhabitants of these countries and territories in such a manner as to lead them to the economic, social and cultural development which they expect.

Article 132

Such association shall have the following objects:

1. Member States shall, in their commercial exchanges with the countries and territories, apply the same rules which they apply among themselves pursuant to this Treaty.

2. Each country or territory shall apply to its commercial exchanges with Member States and with the other countries and territories the same rules which it applies in respect of the European State with which it has special relations.

3. Member States shall contribute to the investments required by the progressive development of these countries and territories.

4. As regards investments financed by the Community, participation in tenders and supplies shall be open, on equal terms, to all natural and legal persons being nationals of Member States or of the countries and territories.

From Secretariat of the Interim Committee for the Common Market and Euratom, *Treaty Establishing the European Economic Community and Connected Documents,* Brussels, 1957.

5. In relations between Member States and the countries and territories, the right of establishment of nationals and companies shall be regulated in accordance with the provisions, and by application of the procedures, referred to in the Chapter relating to the right of establishment and on a non-discriminatory basis, subject to the special provisions made pursuant to Article 136.

Article 133

1. Imports originating in the countries or territories shall, on their entry into Member States, benefit by the total abolition of customs duties which shall take place progressively between Member States in conformity with the provisions of this Treaty.

2. Customs duties imposed on imports from Member States and from countries or territories shall, on the entry of such imports into any of the other countries or territories, be progressively abolished in conformity with the provisions of Articles 12, 13, 14, 15 and 17.

3. The countries and territories may, however, levy customs duties which correspond to the needs of their development and to the requirements of their industrialisation or which, being of a fiscal nature, have the object of contributing to their budgets.

The duties referred to in the preceding sub-paragraph shall be progressively reduced to the level of those imposed on imports of products coming from the Member State with which each country or territory has special relations. The percentages and the timing of the reductions provided for under this Treaty shall apply to the difference between the duty imposed, on entry into the importing country or territory, on a product coming from the Member State which has special relations with the country or territory concerned and the duty imposed on the same product coming from the Community.

4. Paragraph 2 shall not apply to countries and territories which, by reason of the special international obligations by which they are bound, already apply a non-discriminatory customs tariff at the date of the entry into force of this Treaty.

5. The establishment or amendment of customs duties imposed on goods imported into the countries and territories shall not, either de jure or de facto, give rise to any direct or indirect discrimination between imports coming from the various Member States.

Article 134

If the level of the duties applicable to goods coming from a third country on entry into a country or territory is likely, having regard to the application of the provisions of Article 133, paragraph 1, to cause diversions of commercial traffic to the detriment of any Member State, the latter may request the Commission to propose to the other Member States the measures necessary to remedy the situation.

Article 135

Subject to the provisions relating to public health, public safety and public order, the freedom of movement in Member States of workers from the countries and territories, and in the countries and territories of workers from Member States shall be governed by subsequent conventions which shall require unanimous agreement of Member States.

Article 136

For a first period of five years as from the date of the entry into force of this Treaty, an Implementing Convention annexed to this Treaty shall determine the particulars and procedure concerning the association of the countries and territories with the Community.

Before the expiry of the Convention provided for in the preceding sub-paragraph, the Council, acting by means of a unanimous vote, shall, proceeding from the results achieved and on the basis of the principles set out in this Treaty, determine the provisions to be made for a further period.

PART SIX: GENERAL AND FINAL PROVISIONS

Article 238

The Community may conclude with a third country, a union of States or an international organisation agreements creating an association embodying reciprocal rights and obligations, joint actions and special procedures.

Such agreements shall be concluded by the Council acting by means of a unanimous vote and after consulting the Assembly.

Where such agreements involve amendments to this Treaty, such amendments shall be subject to prior adoption in accordance with the procedure laid down in Article 236.

APPENDIX B
LIST OF ASSOCIATES UNDER
PART IV OF THE TREATY OF ROME

French West Africa including: Senegal, the Sudan, Guinea, the Ivory Coast, Dahomey, Mauretania, the Niger and the Upper Volta;

French Equatorial Africa including: the Middle Congo, Ubangi-Shari, Chad and Gaboon;

St. Pierre and Miquelon, the Comoro Archipelago, Madagascar and dependencies, the French Somali Coast, New Caledonia and dependencies, the French Settlements in Oceania, the Southern and Antarctic Territories;

The Autonomous Republic of Togoland;

The French Trusteeship Territory in the Cameroons;

The Belgian Congo and Ruanda-Urundi;

The Italian Trusteeship Territory in Somaliland; and

Netherlands New Guinea.

From Secretariat of the Interim Committee for the Common Market and Euratom, *Treaty Establishing the European Economic Community and Connected Documents,* Brussels, 1957.

RELEVANT ARTICLES OF THE CONVENTION OF ASSOCIATION (YAOUNDE CONVENTION), 1963

TRADE

Article 1

With a view to promoting an increase of trade between the Associated States and the Member States, strengthening their economic relations and the economic independence of the Associated States and thereby contributing to the development of international trade, the High Contracting Parties have agreed upon the following provisions which shall regulate their mutual trade relations.

Article 2

1. Goods originating in Associated States, shall, when imported into Member States, benefit from the progressive abolition of customs duties and charges having an effect equivalent to such duties, resulting between Member States under the provisions of Articles 12, 13, 14, 15 and 17 of the Treaty and the decisions which have been or may be adopted to accelerate the rate of achieving the aims of the Treaty.

2. Nevertheless, upon the entry into force of the Convention, Member States shall abolish the customs duties and charges having an effect equivalent to such duties which they apply to the goods originating in Associated States which are listed in the Annex to this Convention.

At the same time Member States shall apply the common customs tariff duties of the Community to imports of these goods from third countries.

3. Imports from third countries of unroasted coffee into the Benelux countries on the one hand, and of bananas into the Federal Republic of Germany on the other hand, shall be subject to the terms set out respectively, as to unroasted coffee, in the Protocol this day concluded between the Member States and, as to bananas, in the Protocol concluded on 25 March 1957 between the Member States and in the Declaration annexed to this Convention.

From *E.E.C. and The African Associated States: The Convention of Association,* distributed for the Royal Institute of International Affairs (London: Oxford University Press, 1963).

Article 3

1. Each Associated State shall accord identical tariff treatment to goods originating in any of the Member States; Associated States not applying this rule on the entry into force of this Convention shall do so within the following six months.

2. In each Associated State goods originating in Member States shall benefit, under the terms set out in Protocol No. 1 annexed to this Convention, from the progressive abolition of customs duties and charges having an effect equivalent to such duties which that Associated State applies to imports of these goods into its territory.

Provided always that, each Associated State may retain or introduce customs duties and charges having an effect equivalent to such duties which correspond to its development needs or its industrialization requirements or which are intended to contribute to its budget.

The customs duties and charges having an effect equivalent to such duties levied by Associated States in accordance with the foregoing sub-paragraph, as also any alteration which they may make in these duties and charges under the provisions of Protocol No. 1, may not either de jure or de facto give rise to any direct or indirect discrimination between Member States.

3. At the request of the Community and in accordance with the procedures laid down in Protocol No. 1, there shall be consultations within the Association Council regarding the conditions of application of this Article.

Article 7

Without prejudice to the special provisions for border trade, the treatment that the Associated States apply by virtue of this Title to goods originating in Member States shall in no case be less favourable than that applied to goods originating in the most favoured third country.

Article 8

This Convention shall not preclude the maintenance or establishment of customs unions or free-trade areas among Associated States.

Article 9

This Convention shall not preclude the maintenance or establishment of customs unions or free-trade areas between one or more Associated States and one or more third countries insofar as they neither are nor prove to be incompatible with the principles and provisions of the said Convention.

Article 11

When drawing up its common agricultural policy, the Community shall take the interests of the Associated States into consideration as regards products similar to and competitive with European products. The Community and the Associated States concerned shall consult together for this purpose.

The treatment applicable to imports into the Community of these products, if they have originated in the Associated States, shall be determined by the Community in the course of defining its common agricultural policy, after consultation within the Association Council.

GENERAL

Article 58

1. The Association Council shall be informed of any request made by a State for accession to or association with the Community.

2. There shall be consultations within the Association Council on any request for association with the Community made by a State which has an economic structure and production comparable to those of the Associated States if the Community, after examining the said request, has laid it before the Association Council.

Article 59

This Convention shall be concluded for a period of five years from the date of its entry into force.

APPENDIX D
LOMÉ CONVENTION, 1975

TITLE 1:
Trade Co-operation

Article 1

In the field of trade co-operation, the object of this Convention is to promote trade between the Contracting Parties, taking account of their respective levels of development, and, in particular, of the need to secure additional benefits for the trade of ACP States, in order to accelerate the rate of growth of their trade and improve the conditions of access of their products to the market of the European Economic Community, (hereinafter called the "Community") so as to ensure a better balance in the trade of the Contracting Parties.

To this end the Contracting Parties shall apply Chapters 1 and 2 of this Title.

CHAPTER 1: TRADE ARRANGEMENTS

Article 2

1. Products originating in the ACP States shall be imported into the Community free of customs duties and charges having equivalent effect, but the treatment applied to these products may not be more favourable than that applied by the Member States among themselves.

For the purpose of the first subparagraph the transitional provisions in force relating to the residual customs duties and charges having equivalent effect resulting from the application of Articles 32 and 36 of the Act concerning the Conditions of Accession and the Adjustments to the Treaties shall have no application.

2. (a) Products originating in the ACP States:

— listed in Annex II to the Treaty when they come under a common organization of the market within the meaning of Article 40 of the Treaty, or

— subject, on importation into the Community, to specific rules introduced as a result of the implementation of the common agricultural policy; shall be imported into the Community notwithstanding the general arrangements applied in respect of third countries, in accordance with the following provisions:

(i) those products shall be imported free of customs duties for which Community provisions in force at the time of importation do not provide, apart from customs duties, for the application of any other measure relating to their importation;

(ii) for products other than those referred to under (i), the Community shall take the necessary measures to ensure, as a general rule, more favourable treatment than the general treatment applicable to the same products originating in third countries to which the most-favoured-nation clause applies.

(b) These arrangements shall enter into force at the same time as this Convention and shall remain applicable for its duration.

If, however, during the application of this Convention, the Community,

— subjects one or more products to common organization of the market or to specific rules introduced as a result of the implementation of the common agricultural policy, it reserves the right to adapt the import treatment for these products originating in the ACP States, following consultations within the Council of Ministers. In such cases, paragraph 2(a) shall be applicable;

— modifies the common organization of the market in a particular product or the specific rules introduced as a result of the implementation of the common agricultural policy, it reserves the right to modify the arrangements laid down for products originating in the ACP States, following consultations within the Council of Ministers. In such cases, the Community undertakes to ensure that products originating in the ACP States continue to enjoy an advantage comparable to that previously enjoyed in relation to products originating in third countries benefiting from the most-favoured-nation clause.

Article 3

1. The Community shall not apply to imports of products originating in the ACP States any quantitative restrictions or measures having equivalent effect other than those which the Member States apply among themselves.

2. Paragraph 1, however, shall not prejudice the import treatment applied to the products referred to in the first indent of Article 2(2)(a).

The Community shall inform the ACP States when residual quantitative restrictions are eliminated in respect of any of these products.

3. This Article shall not prejudice the treatment that the Community applies to certain products in implementation of world commodity agreements to which the Community and the ACP States concerned are signatory.

Article 4

Nothing in this Convention shall preclude prohibitions or restrictions on imports, exports or goods in transit justified on grounds of public morality, public policy or public security; the protection of health and life of humans, animals and plants; the protection of national treasures possessing artistic, historic or archaeological value or the protection of industrial and commercial property.

Such prohibitions or restrictions shall not, however, constitute a means of arbitrary discrimination or a disguised restriction on trade.

Article 5

Where new measures or measures stipulated in programmes adopted by the Community for the approximation of laws and regulations in order to facilitate the movement of goods are likely to affect the interests of one or more ACP States the Community shall, prior to adopting such measures, inform the ACP States thereof through the Council of Ministers.

In order to enable the Community to take into consideration the interests of the ACP States concerned, consultations shall be held upon the request of the latter with a view to reaching a satisfactory solution.

Article 6

Where existing rules or regulations of the Community adopted in order to facilitate the movement of goods or where the interpretation, application or administration thereof affect the interests of one or more ACP States, consultations shall be held at the request of the latter with a view to reaching a satisfactory solution.

With a view to finding a satisfactory solution, the ACP States may also bring up within the Council of Ministers any other problems relating to the movement of goods which might result from measures taken or to be taken by the Member States.

The competent institutions of the Community shall to the greatest possible extent inform the Council of Ministers of such measures.

Article 7

1. In view of their present development needs, the ACP States shall not be required, for the duration of this Convention, to assume, in respect of imports of products originating in the Community, obligations corresponding to the commitments entered into by the Community in respect of imports of the products originating in the ACP States, under this Chapter.

2. (a) In their trade with the Community, the ACP States shall not discriminate among the Member States, and shall grant to the Community treatment no less favourable than the most-favoured-nation treatment.

(b) The most-favoured-nation treatment referred to in subparagraph (a) shall not apply in respect of trade or economic relations between ACP States or between one or more ACP States and other developing countries.

Article 8

Each Contracting Party shall communicate its customs tariff to the Council of Ministers within a period of three months following the entry into force of this Convention. It shall also communicate any subsequent amendments to that tariff as and when they occur.

Article 9

1. The concept of "originating products" for the purposes of implementing this Chapter, and the methods of administrative co-operation relating thereto, are laid down in Protocol No 1.

2. The Council of Ministers may adopt any amendment to Protocol No 1.

3. Where the concept of "originating products" has not yet been defined for a given product in implementation of paragraphs 1 or 2, each Contracting Party shall continue to apply its own rules.

Article 10

1. If, as a result of applying the provisions of this Chapter, serious disturbances occur in a sector of the economy of the Community or of one or more of its Member States, or jeopardize their external financial stability, or if difficulties arise which may result in a deterioration in a sector of the economy of a region of the Community, the latter may take, or may authorize the Member State concerned to take, the necessary safeguard measures. These measures and the methods of applying them shall be notified immediately to the Council of Ministers.

2. For the purpose of implementing paragraph 1, priority shall be given to such measures as would least disturb the trade relations between the Contracting Parties and the attainment of the objectives of the Convention. These

measures shall not exceed the limits of what is strictly necessary to remedy the
difficulties that have arisen.

Article 11

In order to ensure effective implementation of the provisions of this
Convention in the field of trade co-operation, the Contracting Parties agree to
inform and consult each other.

Consultations shall take place, at the request of the Community or of the
ACP States, in accordance with the conditions provided for in the rules of
procedure in Article 74, particularly in the following cases:

1. Where Contracting Parties envisage taking any trade measures affecting the interest of one or more Contracting Parties under this Convention, they
shall inform the Council of Ministers thereof. Consultations shall take place,
where the Contracting Parties concerned so request, in order to take into
account their respective interests.

2. Where the Community envisages concluding a preferential trade
agreement it shall inform the ACP States thereof. Consultations shall
take place, where the ACP States so request, in order to safeguard their
interests.

3. Where the Community or the Member States take safeguard measures
in accordance with Article 10, consultations on these measures may take place
within the Council of Ministers, where the Contracting Parties concerned so
request, notably with a view to ensuring compliance with Article 10(2).

4. If, during the application of this Convention, the ACP States consider
that agricultural products covered by Article 2(2)(a), other than those subject
to special treatment, call for special treatment, consultations may take place
within the Council of Ministers.

CHAPTER 2: TRADE PROMOTION

Article 12

With a view of attaining the objectives they have set themselves as regards
trade and industrial co-operation the Contracting Parties shall carry out trade
promotion activities which will be aimed at helping the ACP States to derive
maximum benefit from Title I. Chapter 1 and Title III and to participate under
the most favourable conditions in the Community, regional and international
markets.

Article 13

The trade promotion activities provided for in Article 12 shall include:

(a) improving the structure and working methods of organizations, departments or firms contributing to the development of the foreign trade of ACP States, or setting up such organizations, departments or firms;

(b) basic training or advanced vocational training of staff in trade promotion;

(c) participation by the ACP States in fairs, exhibitions, specialized international shows and the organization of trade events;

(d) improving co-operation between economic operators in the Member States and the ACP States and establishing links to promote such co-operation;

(e) carrying out and making use of market research and marketing studies;

(f) producing and distributing trade information in various forms within the Community and the ACP States with a view to developing trade.

Article 14

Applications for financing of trade promotion activities shall be presented to the Community by the ACP State or ACP States concerned under the conditions laid down in Title IV.

Article 15

The Community shall participate, under the conditions laid down in Title IV and in Protocol No 2, in financing trade promotion activities for promoting the development of exports of ACP States.

TITLE II:
Export Earnings from Commodities

CHAPTER 1: STABILIZATION OF EXPORT EARNINGS

Article 16

With the aim of remedying the harmful effects of the instability of export earnings and of thereby enabling the ACP States to achieve the stability, profitability and sustained growth of their economies, the Community shall implement a system for guaranteeing the stabilization of earnings from exports by the ACP States to the Community of certain products on which their economies are dependent and which are affected by fluctuations in price and/ or quantity.

Article 17

1. Export earnings to which the stabilization system applies shall be those accruing from the exportation by the ACP States to the Community of the products on the following list, drawn up taking account of factors such as employment, deterioration of the terms of trade between the Community and the ACP State concerned, the level of development of the State concerned and the particular difficulties of the least developed, landlocked or island ACP States listed in Article 24:

- a. Groundnut products
    - (aa) groundnuts, shelled or not
    - (ab) groundnut oil
    - (ac) groundnut oilcake
- b. Cocoa products
    - (ba) cocoa beans
    - (bb) cocoa paste
    - (bc) cocoa butter
- c. Coffee products
    - (ca) raw or roasted coffee
    - (cb) extracts, essences or concentrates of coffee
- d. Cotton products
    - (da) cotton, not carded or combed
    - (db) cotton linters
- e. Coconut products
    - (ea) coconuts
    - (eb) copra
    - (ec) coconut oil
    - (ed) coconut oilcake
- f. Palm, palm nut and kernel products
    - (fa) palm oil
    - (fb) palm nut and kernel oil
    - (fc) palm nut and kernel oilcake
    - (fd) palm nuts and kernels
- g. Raw hides, skins and leather
    - (ga) raw hides and skins
    - (gb) bovine cattle leather

    (gc) sheep and lamb skin leather

    (gd) goat and kid skin leather

h. Wood products

    (ha) wood in the rough

    (hb) wood roughly squared or half-squared, but not further manufac-
        tured

    (hc) wood sawn lengthwise, but not further prepared

i. Fresh bananas

k. Tea

l. Raw sisal

m. Iron ore

Iron ores and concentrates and roasted iron pyrites.

The statistics used for implementation of the system shall be those obtained by cross-checking the statistics of the ACP States and of the Community, account being taken of the fob values.

The system shall be implemented in respect of the products listed above where they are:

    (a) released for home use in the Community;

    (b) brought under the inward processing arrangements there in order to be processed.

2. The system shall apply to an ACP State's export earnings from the products listed above if, during the year preceding the year of application, earnings from the export of the product or products to all destinations represented at least 7.5% of its total earnings from merchandise exports: for sisal, however, the percentage shall be 5%. For the least developed, landlocked or island ACP States listed in Article 24 the percentage shall be 2.5%.

3. Nonetheless if, not sooner than 12 months following the entry into force of this Convention, one or more products not contained in this list, but upon which the economies of one or more ACP States depend to a considerable extent, are affected by sharp fluctuations, the Council of Ministers may decide whether the product or products should be included in the list, without prejudice to Article 18(1).

4. For certain special cases the system shall apply to exports of the products in question irrespective of destination.

5. The ACP States concerned shall certify that the products to which the stabilization system applies have originated in their territory.

Article 18

1. For the purposes specified in Article 16 and for the duration of this Convention, the Community shall allocate to the stabilization system a total amount of 375 million units of account to cover all its commitments under the

said system. This amount shall be managed by the Commission of the European Communities (hereinafter called the "Commission").

2. This total amount shall be divided into five equal annual instalments. Every year except the last, the Council of Ministers may authorize, where required, the use in advance of a maximum of 20% of the following year's instalment.

3. Whatever balance remains at the end of each year of the first four years of the application of this Convention shall be carried forward automatically to the following year.

4. On the basis of a report submitted to it by the Commission, the Council of Ministers may reduce the amount of the transfers to be made under the stabilization system.

5. Before the expiry of this Convention, the Council of Ministers shall decide on the use to which any balance remaining from the total amount referred to in paragraph 1 is to be put and also on the terms to be laid down for the further use of amounts still to be paid by the ACP States, under Article 21, after the expiry of this convention.

Article 19

1. In order to implement the stabilization system a reference level shall be calculated for each ACP State and for each product.

This reference level shall correspond to the component of export earnings during the four years preceding each year of application.

2. An ACP State shall be entitled to request a financial transfer if, on the basis of the results of a calendar year, its actual earnings, as defined in Article 17, from each of the products considered individually, are at least 7.5% below the reference level. For the least developed, landlocked or island ACP States listed in Article 24 the percentage shall be 2.5%

3. The request from the ACP State concerned shall be addressed to the Commission, which shall examine it in the light of the volume of resources available.

The difference between the reference level and actual earnings shall constitute the basis of the transfer.

4. However,

(a) should examination of the request, to be undertaken by the Commission in conjunction with the ACP State concerned, show that the fall in earnings from exports to the Community of the products in question is the result of a trade policy measure of the ACP State concerned adversely affecting exports to the Community in particular, the request shall not be admissible;

(b) should examination of the total exports of the requesting ACP State show a significant change, consultations shall be held between the Commission and the requesting State to determine whether such changes are likely to have an effect on the amount of the transfer, and if so to what extent.

5. Except in the case referred to in paragraph 4(a) the Commission shall, in conjunction with the requesting ACP State, draw up a draft decision to make a transfer.

6. All necessary steps shall be taken to ensure that transfers are made rapidly, for example by means of advances, normally six-monthly.

Article 20

The recipient ACP State shall decide how the resources will be used. It shall inform the Commission annually of the use to which it has put the resources transferred.

Article 21

1. The amounts transferred shall not bear interest.

2. The ACP States which have received transfers shall contribute, in the five years following the allocation of each transfer, towards the reconstitution of the resources made available for the system by the Community.

3. Each ACP State shall help reconstitute the resources when it is found that the trend of its export earnings will so permit.

To this effect, the Commission shall determine, for each year and for each product, and on the conditions specified in Article 17(1), whether

— the unit value of the exports is higher than the reference unit value;

— the quantity actually exported to the Community is at least equal to the reference quantity.

If the two conditions are met at the same time, the recipient ACP State shall pay back into the system, within the limit of the transfers it has received, an amount equal to the reference quantity multiplied by the difference between the reference unit value and the actual unit value.

4. If, on expiry of the five-year period referred to in paragraph 2, the resources have not been fully reconstituted, the Council of Ministers, taking into consideration in particular the situation of and prospects for the balance of payments, exchange reserves and foreign indebtedness of the ACP States concerned, may decide that:

— the sums outstanding are to be reconstituted wholly or partially, in one or more instalments;

— rights to repayment are to be waived.

5. Paragraphs 2, 3 and 4 shall not apply to the ACP States listed in Article 48.

Article 22

For each transfer a "transfer agreement" shall be drawn up and concluded between the Commission and the ACP State concerned.

Article 23

1. In order to ensure that the stabilization system functions efficiently and rapidly, statistical and customs co-operation shall be instituted between the Community and the ACP States. The detailed arrangements for such co-operation shall be established by the Council of Ministers.
2. The ACP States and the Commission shall adopt by mutual agreement any practical measures facilitating the exchange of necessary information and the submission of requests for transfers, for example by producing a form for requesting transfers.

Article 24

The least developed, landlocked or island ACP States referred to in Article 17(1) and (2) and Article 19(2) are as follows:

the Bahamas	Malawi
Barbados	Mali
Botswana	Mauritania
Burundi	Mauritius
Central African Republic	Niger
Chad	Rwanda
Dahomey	Somalia
Equatorial Guinea	Sudan
Ethiopia	Swaziland
Fiji	Tanzania
the Gambia	Togo
Grenada	Tonga
Guinea	Trinidad and Tobago
Guinea-Bissau	Uganda
Jamaica	Upper Volta
Lesotho	Western Samoa
Madagascar	Zambia

CHAPTER 2: SPECIFIC PROVISIONS CONCERNING SUGAR

Article 25

1. Notwithstanding any other provisions of this Convention the Community undertakes for an indefinite period to purchase and import, at guaranteed prices, specific quantities of cane sugar, raw or white, which originate in the ACP States producing and exporting cane sugar and which those States undertake to deliver to it.

2. Protocol No 3 annexed to this Convention determines the conditions of implementation of this Article.

TITLE III:
Industrial Co-operation

Article 26

The Community and the ACP States, acknowledging the pressing need for the industrial development of the latter, agree to take all measures necessary to bring about effective industrial co-operation.

Industrial co-operation between the Community and the ACP States shall have the following objectives:

(a) to promote the development and diversification of industry in the ACP States and to help bring about a better distribution of industry both within those States and between them;

(b) to promote new relations in the industrial field between the Community, its Member States and the ACP States, in particular the establishment of new industrial and trade links between the industries of the Member States and those of the ACP States;

(c) to increase the links between industry and the other sectors of the economy, in particular agriculture;

(d) to facilitate the transfer of technology to the ACP States and to promote the adaptation of such technology to their specific conditions and needs, for example by expanding the capacity of the ACP States for research, for adaptation of technology and for training in industrial skills at all levels in these States;

(e) to promote the marketing of industrial products of the ACP States in foreign markets in order to increase their share of international trade in those products;

(f) to encourage the participation of nationals of ACP States, in particular that of small and medium-sized industrial firms, in the industrial development of those States;

(g) to encourage Community firms to participate in the industrial development of the ACP States, where those States so desire and in accordance with their economic and social objectives.

Article 27

In order to attain the objectives set out in Article 26, the Community shall help to carry out, by all the means provided for in the Convention, programmes, projects and schemes submitted to it on the initiative or with the agreement of the ACP States in the fields of industrial infrastructures and ventures, training, technology and research, small and medium-sized firms, industrial information and promotion, and trade co-operation.

Article 28

The Community shall contribute to the setting up and the extension of the infrastructure necessary for industrial development, particularly in the fields of transport and communications, energy and industrial research and training.

Article 29

The Community shall contribute to the setting up and the extension in the ACP States of industries processing raw materials and industries manufacturing finished and semi-finished products.

Article 30

At the request of the ACP States and on the basis of the programmes submitted by the latter, the Community shall contribute to the organization and financing of the training, at all levels, of personnel of the ACP States in industries and institutions within the Community.

In addition, the Community shall contribute to the establishment and expansion of industrial training facilities in the ACP States.

Article 31

With a view to helping the ACP States to overcome obstacles encountered by them in matters of access to and adaptation of technology, the Community is prepared in particular to:

(a) keep the ACP States better informed on technological matters and assist them in selecting the technology best adapted to their needs;

(b) facilitate their contacts and relations with firms and institutions in possession of the appropriate technological know-how;

(c) facilitate the acquisition, on favourable terms and conditions, of patents and other industrial property, in particular through financing and/or through other suitable arrangements with firms and institutions within the Community;

(d) contribute to the establishment and expansion of industrial research facilities in the ACP States with particular reference to the adaptation of available technology to the conditions and needs of those States.

Article 32

The Community shall contribute to the establishment and development of small and medium-sized industrial firms in the ACP States through financial and technical co-operation schemes adapted to the specific needs of such firms and covering inter alia:

(a) the financing of firms,

(b) the creation of appropriate infrastructure and industrial estates,

(c) vocational and advanced training,

(d) the setting up of specialized advisory services and credit facilities.

The development of these firms shall, as far as possible, be conducive to the strengthening of the complementary relationship between small and medium-sized industrial firms and of their links with large industrial firms.

Article 33

Industrial information and promotion schemes shall be carried out in order to secure and intensify regular information exchanges and the necessary contacts in the industrial field between the Community and the ACP States.

These schemes could have the following aims:

(a) to gather and disseminate all relevant information on the trends of industry and trade in the Community and on the conditions and possibilities for industrial development in the ACP States;

(b) to organize and facilitate contacts and meetings of all kinds between Community and ACP States' industrial policy-makers, promoters and firms;

(c) to carry out studies and appraisals aimed at pinpointing the practical opportunities for industrial co-operation with the Community in order to promote the industrial development of the ACP States;

(d) to contribute, through appropriate technical co-operation schemes, to the setting up, launching and running of the ACP States' industrial promotion bodies.

Article 34

In order to enable the ACP States to obtain full benefit from trade and other arrangements provided for in this Convention, trade promotion schemes shall be carried out to encourage the marketing of industrial products of ACP States both in the Community as well as in other external markets. Furthermore, programmes shall be drawn up jointly between the Community and the ACP States in order to stimulate and develop the trade of industrial products among the said States.

Article 35

1. A Committee on Industrial Co-operation shall be established. It shall be supervised by the Committee of Ambassadors.

2. The Committee on Industrial Co-operation shall:

(a) see to the implementation of this Title;

(b) examine the problems in the field of industrial co-operation submitted to it by the ACP States and/or by the Community, and suggest appropriate solutions;

(c) guide, supervise and control the activities of the Centre for Industrial Development referred to in Article 36 and report to the Committee of Ambassadors and, through it, to the Council of Ministers;

(d) submit from time to time reports and recommendations which it considers appropriate to the Committee of Ambassadors;

(e) perform such other functions as may be assigned to it by the Committee of Ambassadors.

3. The composition of the Committee on Industrial Co-operation and the details for its operation shall be determined by the Council of Ministers.

Article 36

A Centre for Industrial Development shall be set up. It shall have the following functions:

(a) to gather and disseminate in the Community and the ACP States all relevant information on the conditions of and opportunities for industrial co-operation;

(b) to have, at the request of the Community and the ACP States, studies carried out on the possibilities and potential for industrial development of the ACP States, bearing in mind the necessity for adaptation of technology to their needs and requirements, and to ensure their follow-up;

(c) to organize and facilitate contacts and meetings of all kinds between Community and ACP States' industrial policy-makers, promoters, and firms and financial institutions;

(d) to provide specific industrial information and support services;

(e) help to identify, on the basis of needs indicated by ACP States, the opportunities for industrial training and applied research in the Community and in the ACP States, and to provide relevant information and recommendations.

The Centre's Statutes and rules of operation shall be adopted by the Council of Ministers on a proposal from the Committee of Ambassadors upon the entry into force of this Convention.

Article 37

Programmes, projects or schemes undertaken in the field of industrial co-operation and involving Community financing shall be implemented in accordance with Title IV, taking into account the particular characteristics of interventions in the industrial sector.

Article 38

1. Each ACP State shall endeavour to give as clear an indication as possible of its priority areas for industrial co-operation and the form it would like such co-operation to take. It will also take such steps as are necessary to promote effective co-operation within the framework of this Title with the Community and the Member States or with firms or nationals of Member States who comply with the development programmes and priorities of the host ACP State.

2. The Community and its Member States, for their part, shall endeavour to set up measures to attract the participation of their firms and nationals in the industrial development efforts of the ACP States concerned, and shall encourage such firms and nationals to adhere to the aspirations and development objectives of those ACP States.

Article 39

This Title shall not prevent any ACP State or groups of ACP States from entering into specific arrangements for the development in ACP States of agricultural, mineral, energy and other specific resources with a Member State or States of the Community, provided that these arrangements are compatible with this Convention. Such arrangements must be complementary to the efforts on industrialization and must not operate to the detriment of this Title.

TITLE IV:
Financial and Technical Co-operation

Article 40

1. The purpose of economic, financial and technical co-operation is to correct the structural imbalances in the various sectors of the ACP States' economies. The co-operation shall relate to the execution of projects and programmes which contribute essentially to the economic and social development of the said States.

2. Such development shall consist in particular in the greater well-being of the population, improvement of the economic situation of the State, local authorities and firms, and the introduction of structures and factors whereby such improvement can be continued and extended by their own means.

3. This co-operation shall complement the efforts of the ACP States and shall be adapted to the characteristics of each of the said States.

Article 41

1. The Council of Ministers shall examine at least once a year whether the objectives referred to in Article 40 are being attained and shall also examine the general problems resulting from the implementation of financial and technical co-operation. It shall take stock, on the basis of information gathered both by the Community and the ACP States, of action undertaken in this context by the Community and by the ACP States. This stocktaking shall also cover regional co-operation and measures in favour of the least developed ACP States.

As regards the Community, the Commission shall submit to the Council of Ministers an annual report on the management of Community financial and technical aid. This report shall be drawn up in collaboration with the European Investment Bank (hereinafter called the "Bank") for the parts of the report which concern it. It shall in particular show the position as to the commitment, implementation and utilization of the aid, broken down by type of financing and by recipient State.

The ACP States for their part shall submit to the Council of Ministers any observations, information or proposals on the problems concerning the implementation, in their respective countries, of the economic, financial and technical co-operation, and also on the general work problems of this co-operation.

The work on the annual stocktaking of financial and technical co-operation shall be prepared by the experts of the Community and of the ACP States who are responsible for the implementation of that co-operation.

2. On the basis of the information submitted by the Community and the ACP States and of the examination referred to in paragraph 1, the Council of Ministers shall define the policy and guidelines of financial and technical co-operation and shall formulate resolutions on the measures to be taken by the Community and the ACP States in order to ensure that the objectives of such co-operation are attained.

Article 42

For the duration of this Convention, the overall amount of the Community's aid shall be 3,390 million units of account.

This amount comprises:

1. 3,000 million units of account from the European Development Fund (hereinafter called the "Fund"), allocated as follows:

(a) for the purposes set out in Article 40: 2,625 million units of account, consisting of:

— 2,100 million units of account in the form of grants,

— 430 million units of account in the form of special loans,

— 95 million units of account in the form of risk capital;

(b) for the purposes set out in Title II, up to 375 million units of account, likewise from the Fund, in the form of transfers for the stabilization of export earnings.

2. For the purposes set out in Article 40, up to 390 million units of account in the form of loans from the Bank, made from its own resources on the terms and conditions provided for in its Statute, and supplemented, as a general rule, by a 3% interest rate subsidy, under the conditions laid down in Article 5 of Protocol No 2.

The total cost of the interest rate subsidies shall be charged against the amounts of aid provided for in 1 (a) above.

Article 43

1. The method or methods of financing which may be contemplated for each project or programme shall be selected jointly by the Community and the ACP State or States concerned with a view to the best possible use being made of the resources available and by reference to the level of development and the economic and financial situation of the ACP State or ACP States concerned.

Moreover, account shall be taken of the factors which ensure the servicing of repayable aid.

The definitive choice of methods of financing for projects and programmes shall be made only at an appropriate stage in the appraisal of such projects and programmes.

2. Account shall also be taken of the nature of the project or programme, of its prospects of economic and financial profitability and of its economic and social impact.

In particular, productive capital projects in the industrial, tourism and mining sectors shall be given priority financing by means of loans from the Bank and risk capital.

Article 44

1. Where appropriate, a number of methods may be combined for financing a project or programme.

2. With the agreement of the ACP State or ACP States concerned, financial aid from the Community may take the form of co-financing with participation by, in particular, credit and development agencies and institutions, firms, Member States, ACP States, third countries or international finance organizations.

Article 45

1. Grants and special loans may be made available to or through the ACP State concerned.

2. Where these funds are on-lent through the ACP State concerned, the terms and procedure for the onlending by the intermediate recipient to the final borrower shall be laid down between the Community and the State concerned in an intermediate financing agreement.

3. Any benefits accruing to the intermediate recipient, either because that recipient receives a grant or a loan for which the interest rate or the repayment period is more favourable than that of the final loan, shall be employed by the intermediate recipient for the purposes and on the terms set out in the intermediate financing agreement.

Article 46

1. The financing of projects and programmes comprises the means required for their execution, such as:

— capital projects in the fields of rural development, industrialization, energy, mining, tourism, and economic and social infrastructure;

— schemes to improve the structure of agricultural production;

— technical co-operation schemes, in particular in the fields of training and technological adaptation or innovation;

— industrial information and promotion schemes;

— marketing and sales promotion schemes;

— specific schemes to help small and medium-sized national firms;

— microprojects for grassroots development, in particular in rural areas.

2. Financial and technical co-operation shall not cover current administrative, maintenance and operating expenses.

3. Financial aid may cover import costs and local expenditure required for the execution of projects and programmes.

Article 47

1. In the implementation of financial and technical co-operation, the Community shall provide effective assistance for attaining the objectives which the ACP States set themselves in the context of regional and interregional co-operation. This assistance shall aim to:

(a) accelerate economic co-operation and development both within and between the regions of the ACP States;

(b) accelerate diversification of the economies of the ACP States;

(c) reduce the economic dependence of the ACP States on imports by maximizing output of those products for which the ACP States in question have real potential;

(d) create sufficiently wide markets within the ACP States and neighbouring States by removing the obstacles which hinder the development and integration of those markets in order to promote trade between the ACP States;

(e) maximize the use of resources and services in the ACP States.

2. To this end approximately 10% of the total financial resources provided for in Article 42 for the economic and social development of the ACP States shall be reserved for financing their regional projects.

Article 48

1. In the implementation of financial and technical co-operation, special attention shall be paid to the needs of the least developed ACP States so as to reduce the specific obstacles which impede their development and prevent

them from taking full advantage of the opportunities offered by financial and technical co-operation.

2. The following ACP States shall be eligible, according to their particular needs, for the special measures established under this Article:

Botswana	Mauritania
Burundi	Niger
Central African Republic	Rwanda
Chad	Somalia
Dahomey	Sudan
Ethiopia	Swaziland
the Gambia	Tanzania
Guinea	Togo
Guinea-Bissau	Tonga
Lesotho	Uganda
Malawi	Upper Volta
Mali	Western Samoa

3. The list of ACP States in paragraph 2 may be amended by decision of the Council of Ministers:

— where a third State in a comparable economic situation accedes to this Convention;

— where the economic situation of an ACP State undergoes a radical and lasting change either so as to necessitate the application of special measures or so that this treatment is no longer warranted.

Article 49

1. The following shall be eligible for financial and technical co-operation:
(a) the ACP States;
(b) the regional or interstate bodies to which the ACP States belong and which are authorized by the said States;
(c) the joint bodies set up by the Community and the ACP States and authorized by the latter to attain certain specific objectives, notably in the field of industrial and trade co-operation.

2. Subject to the agreement of the ACP State or ACP States concerned, the following shall be eligible for such co-operation in respect of projects or programmes approved by the latter:
(a) local authorities and public or semi-public development agencies of the ACP States, in particular their development banks;
(b) private bodies working in the countries concerned for the economic and social development of the population of those ACP States;

(c) firms carrying out their activities, in accordance with industrial and business management methods, which are set up as companies or firms of an ACP State within the meaning of Article 63

(d) groups of producers that are nationals of the ACP States or like bodies, and, where no such groups or bodies exist, the producers themselves;

(e) for training purposes, scholarship holders and trainees.

Article 50

1. There shall be close co-operation between the Community and the ACP States in implementing aid measures financed by the former. This co-operation shall be achieved through active participation by the ACP State or group of ACP States concerned in each of the various stages of a project: the aid programming, the submission and appraisal of projects, the preparation of financing decisions, execution of projects and final evaluation of the results, in accordance with the various procedures laid down in Articles 51 to 57.

2. As regards project financing for which the Bank is responsible, application of the principles defined in Articles 51 to 58 may be adapted, in concert with the ACP State or ACP States concerned, to take account of the nature of the operations financed and of the Bank's procedures under its Statute.

Article 51

1. Community aid, which is complementary to the ACP States' own efforts, shall be integrated in the economic and social development plans and programmes of the said States so that projects undertaken with the financial support of the Community dovetail with the objectives and priorities set up by those States.

2. At the beginning of the period covered by this Convention, Community aid shall be programmed, in conjunction with each recipient State in such a way that the latter can obtain as clear an idea as possible of the aid, in particular as regards the amount and terms, it can expect during that period and especially for specific objectives which this aid may meet. This programme shall be drawn up on the basis of proposals made by each ACP State, in which it has fixed its objectives and priorities. Projects or programmes already identified on an indicative basis may be the subject of a provisional timetable as regards preparation.

3. The Community indicative aid programme for each ACP State shall be drawn up by mutual agreement by the competent bodies of the Community

and those of the ACP State concerned. It shall then be the subject of an exchange of views, at the beginning of the period covered by this Convention, between the representatives of the Community and those of the ACP State concerned.

This exchange of views shall enable the ACP State to set out its development policy and priorities.

4. The aid programmes shall be sufficiently flexible to enable account to be taken of changes occurring in the economic situation of the various ACP States, and any modifications of their initial priorities. Therefore, each programme may be reviewed whenever necessary during the period covered by this Convention.

5. These programmes shall not cover the exceptional aid referred to in Article 59 or the measures for stabilizing export earnings referred to in Title II.

Article 52

1. Preparation of the projects and programmes which come within the framework of the Community aid programme drawn up by mutual agreement shall be the responsibility of the ACP States concerned or of other beneficiaries approved by them. The Community may, where those States so request, provide technical assistance for drawing up the dossiers of projects or programmes.

2. Such dossiers shall be submitted to the Community as and when they are ready by the beneficiaries specified in Article 49(1), or, with the express agreement of the ACP state or ACP States concerned, by those specified in Article 49(2).

Article 53

1. The Community shall appraise projects and programmes in close collaboration with the ACP States and any other beneficiaries. The technical, social, economic, trade, financial, organizational and management aspects of such projects or programmes shall be reviewed systematically.

2. The aim of appraisal is:

(a) to ensure that the projects and programmes stem from economic or social development plans or programmes of the ACP States;

(b) to assess, as far as possible by means of an economic evaluation, the effectiveness of each project or programme by setting the effects it is expected to produce against the resources to be invested in it. In each project the expected effects shall be the practical expression of a number of specific development objectives of the ACP State or ACP States concerned.

On this basis, appraisal shall ensure that, as far as possible, the measures selected constitute the most effective and profitable method of attaining these objectives, taking into account the various constraints on each ACP State;

(c) to verify that the conditions guaranteeing the successful conclusion and the viability of the projects or programmes are met, which involves:

— verifying that the projects as conceived are suitable for bringing about the effects sought and that the means to be used commensurate with the circumstances and resources of the ACP State or region concerned;

— and furthermore guaranteeing that the staff and other means, particularly financial, necessary for operating and maintaining the investments and for covering incidental project costs are actually available. Particular attention shall be paid here to the possibility of the project being managed by national personnel.

Article 54

1. Financing proposals, which summarize the conclusions of the appraisal and are submitted to the Community's decision-making body, shall be drawn up in close collaboration between the competent departments of the Community and those of the ACP State or ACP States concerned.

The final version of each financing proposal shall be transmitted by the competent departments of the Community simultaneously to the Community and to the ACP States concerned.

2. All projects or programmes put forward officially in accordance with Article 52 by an ACP State or ACP States, whether or not selected by the competent departments of the Community, shall be brought to the attention of the Community body responsible for taking financing decisions.

3. Where the Community body responsible for delivering an opinion on projects fails to deliver a favourable opinion, the competent departments of the Community shall consult the representatives of the ACP State or ACP States concerned on further action to be taken, in particular on the advisability of submitting the dossier afresh, possibly in a modified form, to the relevant Community body.

Before that body gives its final opinion, the representatives of the ACP State or ACP States concerned may request a hearing by the representatives of the Community in order to be able to state their grounds for the project.

Should the final opinion delivered by that body not be favourable, the competent departments of the Community shall consult afresh with the representatives of the ACP State or ACP States concerned before deciding whether the project should be submitted as it stands to the Community's decision-making bodies or whether it should be withdrawn or modified.

Article 55

The ACP States, or the other beneficiaries authorized by them, shall be responsible for the execution of projects financed by the Community.

Accordingly, they shall be responsible for negotiating and concluding works and supply contracts and technical co-operation contracts.

Article 56

1. As regards operations financed by the Community, participation in tendering procedures and other procedures for the award of contracts shall be open on equal terms to all natural and legal persons of the Member States and ACP States.

2. Paragraph 1 shall be without prejudice to measures intended to assist construction firms or manufacturing firms of the ACP States concerned, or of another ACP State, to take part in the execution of works contracts or supply contracts.

3. Paragraph 1 does not mean that the funds paid over by the Community must be used exclusively for the purchase of goods or for the remuneration of services in the Member States and in the ACP States.

Any participation by certain third countries in contracts financed by the Community must, however, be of an exceptional nature and be authorized case-by-case by the competent body of the Community, account being taken in particular of a desire to avoid excessive increases in the cost of projects attributable either to the distances involved and transport difficulties or to the delivery dates.

Participation by third countries may also be authorized where the Community participates in the financing of regional or interregional co-operation schemes involving third countries and in the joint financing of projects with other providers of funds.

Article 57

1. The effects and results of completed projects, and the physical state of the work carried out, shall be evaluated regularly and jointly by the competent departments of the Community and of the ACP State or ACP States concerned in order to ensure that the objectives set are attained under the best conditions.

Evaluations may also be made of projects in progress where this is warranted by their nature, importance or difficulty of execution.

2. The competent institutions of the Community and of the ACP States concerned shall, each for their respective parts, take the measures which evaluation shows to be necessary. The Council of Ministers shall be kept informed of such measures by the Commission and each ACP State for the purposes of Article 41.

Article 58

1. The management and maintenance of work carried out within the context of financial and technical co-operation shall be the responsibility of the ACP States or other beneficiaries.

2. Exceptionally, and by way of derogation from Article 46 (2), in particular under the circumstances specified in Article 10 of Protocol No 2, supplementary aid may be provided temporarily and on a diminishing scale in order to ensure that full use is made of investments which are of special importance for the economic and social development of the ACP State concerned and the running of which temporarily constitutes a truly excessive burden for the ACP State or other beneficiaries.

Article 59

1. Exceptional aid may be accorded to ACP States faced with serious difficulties resulting from natural disasters or comparable extraordinary circumstances.

2. For the purposes of financing the exceptional aid referred to in paragraph 1, a special appropriation shall be constituted within the Fund.

3. The special appropriation shall initially be fixed at 50 million units of account. At the end of each year of application of this Convention this appropriation shall be restored to its initial level.

The total amount of monies transferred from the Fund to the special appropriation during the period of application of the Convention may not exceed 150 million units of account.

Upon expiry of the Convention any monies transferred to the special appropriation which have not been committed for exceptional aid shall be returned to the Fund proper for financing other schemes falling within the field of application of financial and technical co-operation, unless the Council of Ministers decides otherwise.

In the event of the special appropriation being exhausted before the expiry of this Convention, the Community and the ACP States shall adopt, within the relevant joint bodies, appropriate measures to deal with the situations described in paragraph 1.

4. Exceptional aid shall be non-reimbursable. It shall be allocated on a case-by-case basis.

5. Exceptional aid shall help finance the most suitable means of remedying the serious difficulties referred to in paragraph 1.

These means may take the form of works, supplies or provision of services, or cash payments.

6. Exceptional aid shall not be used for dealing with the harmful effects of the instability of export earnings, which are the subject of Title II.

7. The arrangements for allocating exceptional aid, for payments and for implementing the programmes shall be worked out under an emergency procedure, with account being taken of the provisions of Article 54.

Article 60

The fiscal and customs arrangements applicable in the ACP States to contracts financed by the Community shall be adopted by a decision of the Council of Ministers at its first meeting following the date of entry into force of this Convention.

Article 61

In the event of failure of an ACP State to ratify this Convention pursuant to Title VII, or denunciation of this Convention in accordance with that Title, the Contracting Parties shall be obliged to adjust the amounts of the financial aid provided for in this Convention.

TITLE V:
Provisions Relating to Establishment, Services, Payments and Capital Movements

CHAPTER 1: PROVISIONS RELATING TO ESTABLISHMENT AND SERVICES

Article 62

As regards the arrangements that may be applied in matters of establishment and provision of services, the ACP States on the one hand and the

Member States on the other shall treat nationals and companies or firms of Member States and nationals and companies or firms of the ACP States respectively on a non-discriminatory basis. However, if, for a given activity, an ACP State or a Member State is unable to provide such treatment, the Member States or the ACP States, as the case may be, shall not be found to accord such treatment for this activity to the nationals and companies or firms of the State concerned.

Article 63

For the purpose of this Convention "companies or firms" means companies or firms constituted under civil or commercial law, including co-operative societies and other legal persons governed by public or private law, save for those which are non-profit-making.

"Companies or firms of a Member State or of an ACP State" means companies or firms formed in accordance with the law of a Member State or ACP State and whose registered office, central administration or principal place of business is in a Member State or ACP State; however, a company or firm having only its registered office in a Member State or ACP State must be engaged in an activity which has an effective and continuous link with the economy of that Member State or ACP State.

Article 64

At the request of the Community or of the ACP States, the Council of Ministers shall examine any problems raised by the application of Articles 62 and 63. It shall also formulate any relevant recommendations.

CHAPTER 2: PROVISIONS RELATING TO CURRENT PAYMENTS AND CAPITAL MOVEMENTS

Article 65

With regard to capital movements linked with investments and to current payments, the Contracting Parties shall refrain from taking action in the field of foreign exchange transactions which would be incompatible with their

obligations under this Convention resulting from the provisions relating to
trade in goods, to services, establishment and industrial co-operation. These
obligations shall not, however, prevent the Contracting Parties from adopting the necessary protective measures, should this be justified by reasons
relating to serious economic difficulties or severe balance of payments problems.

Article 66

In respect of foreign exchange transactions linked with investments and
current payments, the ACP States on the one hand and the Member States on
the other shall avoid, as far as possible, taking discriminatory measures vis-à-
vis each other or according more favourable treatment to third States, taking
full account of the evolving nature of the international monetary system, the
existence of specific monetary arrangements and balance of payments problems.

To the extent that such measures or treatment are unavoidable they will
be maintained or introduced in accordance with international monetary rules
and every effort will be made to minimize any adverse effects on the Parties
concerned.

Article 67

Throughout the duration of the loans and risk capital operations provided
for in Article 42, each of the ACP States undertakes:
— to place at the disposal of the beneficiaries referred to in Article 49 the
currency necessary for the payment of interest and commission on and amorti-
zation of loans and quasi-capital aid granted for the implementation of aid
measures on their territory;
— to make available to the Bank the foreign exchange necessary for the
transfer of all sums received by it in national currency which represent the net
revenue and proceeds from transactions involving the acquisition by the Community of holdings in the capital of firms.

Article 68

At the request of the Community or of the ACP States, the Council of
Ministers shall examine any problems raised by the application of Articles 65
to 67. It shall also formulate any relevant recommendations.

TITLE VI:
Institutions

Article 69

The Institutions of this Convention are the Council of Ministers, assisted by the Committee of Ambassadors, and the Consultative Assembly.

Article 70

1. The Council of Ministers shall be composed, on the one hand, of the members of the Council of the European Communities and of members of the Commission of the European Communities and, on the other hand, of a member of the Government of each of the ACP States.

2. Any member of the Council of Ministers unable to attend may be represented. The representative shall exercise all the rights of the accredited member.

3. The proceedings of the Council of Ministers shall be valid only if half the members of the Council of the European Communities, one member of the Commission and two thirds of the accredited members representing the Governments of the ACP States are present.

4. The Council of Ministers shall lay down its rules of procedure.

Article 71

The office of President of the Council of Ministers shall be held alternately by a member of the Council of the European Communities and a member of the Government of an ACP State, the latter to be designated by the ACP States.

Article 72

1. Meetings of the Council of Ministers shall be called once a year by its President.

2. The Council of Ministers shall, in addition, meet whenever necessary, in accordance with the conditions laid down in its rules of procedure.

Article 73

1. The Council of Ministers shall act by mutual agreement between the Community on the one hand and the ACP States on the other.

2. The Community on the one hand and the ACP States on the other shall each, by means of an internal protocol, determine the procedure for arriving at their respective positions.

Article 74

1. The Council of Ministers shall define the broad outlines of the work to be undertaken in the context of the application of this Convention.

2. The Council of Ministers shall periodically review the results of the arrangements under this Convention and shall take such measures as may be necessary for the attainment of the objectives of this Convention.

3. Where provided for in this Convention, the Council of Ministers shall have the power to take decisions; such decisions shall be binding on the Contracting Parties, which must take such measures as are required to implement these decisions.

4. The Council of Ministers may likewise formulate such resolutions, recommendations or opinions as it may deem necessary to attain the common objectives and to ensure the smooth functioning of the arrangements of this Convention.

5. The Council of Ministers shall publish an annual report and such other information as it considers appropriate.

6. The Council of Ministers may make all the arrangements that are appropriate for ensuring the maintenance of effective contacts, consultations and co-operation between the economic and social sectors of the Member States and of the ACP States.

7. The Community or the ACP States may raise in the Council of Ministers any problems arising from the application of this Convention.

8. Where provided for in this Convention, consultations shall take place, at the request of the Community or of the ACP States, within the Council of Ministers, in accordance with the conditions laid down in the rules of procedure.

9. The Council of Ministers may set up committees or groups and ad hoc working groups, to undertake such activities as it may determine.

10. At the request of one of the Contracting Parties, exchanges of view may take place on questions having direct repercussions on the matters covered by this Convention.

11. By agreement among the parties, exchanges of views may take place on other economic or technical questions which are of mutual interest.

Article 75

The Council of Ministers may, where necessary, delegate to the Committee of Ambassadors any of its powers. In this event, the Committee of Ambassadors shall give its decisions in accordance with the conditions laid down in Article 73.

Article 76

The Committee of Ambassadors shall be composed, on the one hand, of one representative of each Member State and one representative of the Commission and, on the other, of one representative of each ACP State.

Article 77

1. The Committee of Ambassadors shall assist in the performance of its functions the Council of Ministers shall carry out any mandate entrusted to it by the Council of Ministers.

2. The Committee of Ambassadors shall exercise such other powers and perform such other duties as are assigned to it by the Council of Ministers.

3. The Committee of Ambassadors shall keep under review the functioning of this Convention and the development of the objectives as defined by the Council of Ministers.

4. The Committee of Ambassadors shall account for its actions to the Council of Ministers particularly in matters which have been the subject of delegation of powers. It shall also submit to the Council of Ministers any pertinent proposal and such resolutions, recommendations or opinions as it may deem necessary or consider appropriate.

5. The Committee of Ambassadors shall supervise the work of all the committees and all other bodies or working groups, whether standing or ad hoc, established or provided for by or under this Convention and submit periodical reports to the Council of Ministers.

Article 78

The Office of Chairman of the Committee of Ambassadors shall be held alternately by a representative of a Member State designated by the Community and a representative of an ACP State designated by the ACP States.

The Committee of Ambassadors shall lay down its rules of procedure which shall be submitted to the Council of Ministers for approval.

Article 79

The secretariat duties and other work necessary for the functioning of the Council of Ministers and the Committee of Ambassadors or other joint bodies shall be carried out on a basis of parity and in accordance with the conditions laid down in the rules of procedure of the Council of Ministers.

Article 80

1. The Consultative assembly shall be composed on a basis of parity of members of the Assembly on the side of the Community and of the representatives designated by the ACP States on the other.

2. The Consultative Assembly shall appoint its Bureau and shall adopt its own rules of procedure.

3. The Consultative Assembly shall meet at least once a year.

4. Each year, the Council of Ministers shall submit a report on its activities to the Consultative Assembly.

5. The Consultative Assembly may set up ad hoc consultative committees to undertake such specific activities as it may determine.

6. The Consultative Assembly may adopt resolutions on matters concerning or covered by this Convention.

Article 81

1. Any dispute which arises between one or more Member States or the Community on the one hand, and one or more ACP States on the other, concerning the interpretation or the application of this Convention may be placed before the Council of Ministers.

2. Where circumstances permit, and subject to the Council of Ministers being informed, so that any parties concerned may assert their rights, the Contracting Parties may have recourse to a good offices procedure.

3. If the Council of Ministers fails to settle the dispute at its next meeting, either Party may notify the other of the appointment of an arbitrator; the other Party must then appoint a second arbitrator within two months. For the application of this procedure, the Community and the Member States shall be deemed to be one Party to the dispute.

The Council of Ministers shall appoint a third arbitrator.

The decisions of the arbitrators shall be taken by majority vote.

Each Party to the dispute must take the measures required for the implementation of the arbitrators' decision.

Article 82

The operating expenses of the Institutions under this Convention shall be defrayed in accordance with the terms set out in Protocol No 4 to this Convention.

Article 83

The privileges and immunities for the purpose of this Convention shall be as laid down in Protocol No 5 to this Convention.

TITLE VII:
General and Final Provisions

Article 84

No treaty, convention, agreement or arrangement of any kind between one or more Member States and one or more ACP States may impede the implementation of this Convention.

Article 85

1. This Convention shall apply to the European territories to which the Treaty establishing the European Economic Community applies, in accordance with the conditions set out in that Treaty, on the one hand, and to the territories of the ACP States on the other.

2. Title I of this Convention shall also apply to the relations between the French Overseas Departments and the ACP States.

Article 86

1. As regards the Community, this Convention shall be validly concluded by a decision of the Council of the European Communities taken in accordance with the provisions of the Treaty and notified to the Parties.

It will be ratified by the Signatory States in conformity with their respective constitutional requirements.

2. The instruments of ratification and the act of notification of the conclusion of the Convention shall be deposited, as concerns the ACP States, with

the Secretariat of the Council of the European Communities and, as concerns the Community and its Member States, with the Secretariat of the ACP States. The Secretariats shall forthwith give notice thereof to the Signatory States and the Community.

Article 87

1. This Convention shall enter into force on the first day of the second month following the date of deposit of the instruments of ratification of the Member States and of at least two thirds of the ACP States, and of the act of notification of the conclusion of the Convention by the Community.

2. Any ACP State which has not completed the procedures set out in Article 86 by the date of the entry into force of this Convention as specified in paragraph 1 may do so only within the twelve months following such entry into force and shall be able to proceed with these procedures only during the twelve months following such entry into force, unless before the expiry of this period it gives notice to the Council of Ministers of its intention to complete these procedures not later than six months after this period and on condition that it undertakes the deposit of its instrument of ratification within the same time-limit.

3. As regards those ACP States which have not completed the procedures set out in Article 86 by the date of entry into force of this Convention as specified in paragraph 1, this Convention shall become applicable on the first day of the second month following the completion of the said procedures.

4. Signatory ACP States which ratify this Convention in accordance with the conditions laid down in paragraph 2 shall recognize the validity of all measures taken in implementation of this Convention between the date of its entry into force and the date when its provisions become applicable to them. Subject to any extension which may be granted to them by the Council of Ministers they shall, not later than six months following the completion of the procedures referred to in Article 86, carry out all the obligations of the procedures referred to in Article 86, carry out all the obligations which devolve upon them under the terms of this Convention or of implementing decisions adopted by the Council of Ministers.

5. The rules of procedure of the Institutions set up under this Convention shall lay down whether and under what conditions the representatives of Signatory States which, on the date of entry into force of this Convention have not yet completed the procedures referred to in Article 86, shall sit in those Institutions as observers. The arrangements thus adopted shall be effective only until the date on which this Convention becomes applicable to these States; such arrangements shall in any case cease to apply on the date on

which, pursuant to paragraph 2, the State concerned may no longer ratify the Convention.

Article 88

1. The Council of Ministers shall be informed of any request by any State for membership of, or association with, the Community.

2. The Council of Ministers shall be informed of any request made by any State wishing to become a member of an economic grouping composed of ACP States.

Article 89

1. Any request for accession to this Convention by a country or territory to which Part Four of the Treaty applies, and which becomes independent, shall be referred to the Council of Ministers.

With the approval of the Council of Ministers, the country in question shall accede to this Convention by depositing an instrument of accession with the Secretariat of the Council of the European Communities which shall transmit a certified copy to the Secretariat of the ACP States and shall give notice thereof to the Signatory States.

2. That State shall then enjoy the same rights and be subject to the same obligations as the ACP States. Such accession shall not adversely affect the advantages accruing to the ACP States signatory to this Convention from the provisions on financial and technical cooperation and on the stabilization of export earnings.

Article 90

Any request for accession to this Convention submitted by a State whose economic structure and production are comparable with those of the ACP States shall require approval by the Council of Ministers. The State concerned may accede to this Convention by concluding an agreement with the Community.

That State shall then enjoy the same rights and be subject to the same obligations as the ACP States.

The Agreement may however stipulate the date on which certain of these rights and obligations shall become applicable to that State.

Such accession shall not, however, adversely affect the advantages accruing to the ACP States signatory to this Convention from the provisions on financial and technical co-operation, the stabilization of export earnings and industrial co-operation.

Article 91

This Convention shall expire after a period of five years from the date of its signature, namely 1 March 1980.

Eighteen months before the end of this period the Contracting Parties shall enter into negotiations in order to examine what provisions shall subsequently govern relations between the Community and its Member States and the ACP States.

The Council of Ministers shall adopt any transitional measures that may be required until the new Convention comes into force.

Article 92

This Convention may be denounced by the Community in respect of each ACP State and by each ACP State in respect of the Community, upon six months' notice.

Article 93

The Protocols annexed to this Convention shall form an integral part thereof.

Article 94

This Convention, drawn up in two copies in the Danish, Dutch, English, French, German and Italian languages, all texts being equally authentic, shall be deposited in the archives of the General Secretariat of the Council of the European Communities and the Secretariat of the ACP States which shall both transmit a certified copy to the Government of each of the Signatory States.

RELEVANT ARTICLES OF THE GENERAL AGREEMENT ON TARIFFS AND TRADE, 1947

Article I

General Most-Favoured-Nation Treatment

1. With respect to customs duties and charges of any kind imposed on or in connection with importation or exportation or imposed on the international transfer of payments for imports or exports, and with respect to the method of levying such duties and charges, and with respect to all rules and formalities in connection with importation and exportation, and with respect to all matters referred to in paragraphs 2 and 4 of Article III, any advantage, favour, privilege or immunity granted by any contracting party to any product originating in or destined for any other country shall be accorded immediately and unconditionally to the like product originating in or destined for the territories of all other contracting parties.

2. The provisions of paragraph 1 of this Article shall not require the elimination of any preferences in respect of import duties or charges which do not exceed the levels provided for in paragraph 4 of this Article and which fall within the following descriptions:

(a) Preferences in force exclusively between two or more of the territories listed in Annex A, subject to the conditions set forth therein;

(b) Preferences in force exclusively between two or more territories which on July 1, 1939, were connected by common sovereignty or relations of protection or suzerainty and which are listed in Annexes B, C and D, subject to the conditions set forth therein;

(c) Preferences in force exclusively between the United States of America and the Republic of Cuba;

(d) Preferences in force exclusively between neighbouring countries listed in Annexes E and F.*

3. The provisions of paragraph 1 shall not apply to preferences between the countries formerly a part of the Ottoman Empire and detached from it on

---

*The GATT annexes referred to in Article I list Commonwealth countries, members of the French Union, and other countries benefiting from a preferential system in 1947.

From the General Agreement, as in force on March 1, 1969. Reprinted from Kenneth W. Dam, *The GATT Law and International Economic Organization* (Chicago: University of Chicago Press, 1970), pp. 390–444 passim.

July 24, 1923, provided such preferences are approved under paragraph 5 of Article XXV, which shall be applied in this respect in the light of paragraph 1 of Article XXIX.

4.   The margin of preference on any product in respect of which a preference is permitted under paragraph 2 of this Article but is not specifically set forth as a maximum margin of preference in the appropriate Schedule annexed to this Agreement shall not exceed:

(a) in respect of duties or charges on any product described in such Schedule, the difference between the most-favoured-nation and preferential rates provided for therein; if no preferential rate is provided for, the preferential rate shall for the purposes of this paragraph be taken to be that in force on April 10, 1947, and, if no most-favoured-nation rate is provided for, the margin shall not exceed the difference between the most-favoured-nation and preferential rates existing on April 10, 1947;

(b) in respect of duties or charges on any product not described in the appropriate Schedule, the difference between the most-favoured-nation and preferential rates existing on April 10, 1947.

In the case of the contracting parties named in Annex G, the date of April 10, 1947, referred to in sub-paragraphs (a) and (b) of this paragraph shall be replaced by the respective dates set forth in that Annex.

Article XXIV

Territorial Application-Frontier Traffic-Customs Unions and Free-trade Areas

4.   The contracting parties recognize the desirability of increasing freedom of trade by the development, through voluntary agreements, of closer integration between the economies of the countries parties to such agreements. They also recognize that the purpose of a customs union or of a free-trade area should be to facilitate trade between the constituent territories and not to raise barriers to the trade of other contracting parties with such territories.

5.   Accordingly, the provisions of this Agreement shall not prevent, as between the territories of contracting parties, the formation of a customs union or of a free-trade area or the adoption of an interim agreement necessary for the formation of a customs union or of a free-trade area; Provided that:

(a) with respect to a customs union, or an interim agreement leading to the formation of a customs union, the duties and other regulations of commerce imposed at the institution of any such union or interim agreement in respect of trade with contracting parties not parties to such union or agreement shall not on the whole be higher or more restrictive than the general incidence of the duties and regulations of commerce applicable in the constituent territories prior to the formation of such union or the adoption of such interim agreement, as the case may be;

(b) with respect to a free-trade area, or an interim agreement leading to the formation of a free-trade area, the duties and other regulations of commerce maintained in each of the constituent territories and applicable at the formation of such free-trade area or the adoption of such interim agreement to the trade of contracting parties not included in such area or not parties to such agreement shall not be higher or more restrictive than the corresponding duties and other regulations of commerce existing in the same constituent territories prior to the formation of the free-trade area, or interim agreement, as the case may be; and

(c) any interim agreement referred to in sub-paragraphs (a) and (b) shall include a plan and schedule for the formation of such a customs union or of such a free-trade area within a reasonable length of time.

6. If, in fulfilling the requirements of sub-paragraph 5(a), a contracting party proposes to increase any rate of duty inconsistently with the provisions of Article II, the procedure set forth in Article XXVIII shall apply. In providing for compensatory adjustment, due account shall be taken of the compensation already afforded by the reductions brought about in the corresponding duty of the other constituents of the union.

7. (a) Any contracting party deciding to enter into a customs union or free-trade area, or an interim agreement leading to the formation of such a union or area, shall promptly notify the CONTRACTING PARTIES and shall make available to them such information regarding the proposed union or area as will enable them to make such reports and recommendations to contracting parties as they made deem appropriate.

(b) If, after having studied the plan and schedule included in an interim agreement referred to in paragraph 5 in consultation with the parties to that agreement and taking due account of the information made available in accordance with the provisions of sub-paragraph (a), the CONTRACTING PARTIES find that such agreement is not likely to result in the formation of a customs union or of a free-trade area within the period contemplated by the parties to the agreement or that such period is not a reasonable one, the CONTRACTING PARTIES shall make recommendations to the parties to the agreement. The parties shall not maintain or put into force, as the case may be, such agreement if they are not prepared to modify it in accordance with these recommendations.

(c) Any substantial change in the plan or schedule referred to in paragraph 5(c) shall be communicated to the CONTRACTING PARTIES, which may request the contracting parties concerned to consult with them if the change seems likely to jeopardize or delay unduly the formation of the customs union or of the free-trade area.

8. For the purposes of this Agreement:

(a) A customs union shall be understood to mean the substitution of a single customs territory for two or more customs territories, so that

> (i) duties and other restrictive regulations of commerce (except, where necessary, those permitted under Articles XI, XII, XIII, XIV, XV and XX) are eliminated with respect to substantially all the trade between the constituent territories of the union or at least with respect to substantially all the trade in products originating in such territories, and,
>
> (ii) subject to the provisions of paragraph 9, substantially the same duties and other regulations of commerce are applied by each of the members of the union to the trade of territories not included in the union;

(b) A free-trade area shall be understood to mean a group of two or more customs territories in which the duties and other restrictive regulations of commerce (except, where necessary, those permitted under Articles XI, XII, XIII, XIV, XV and XX) are eliminated on substantially all the trade between the constituent territories in products originating in such territories.

Article XXXV

Non-application of the Agreement between particular Contracting Parties

1. This Agreement, or alternatively Article II of this Agreement, shall not apply as between any contracting party and any other contracting party if:

(a) the two contracting parties have not entered into tariff negotiations with each other, and

(b) either of the contracting parties, at the time either becomes a contracting party, does not consent to such application.

2. The CONTRACTING PARTIES may review the operation of this Article in particular cases at the request of any contracting party and make appropriate recommendations.

TRADE AND DEVELOPMENT

Article XXXVI

Principles and Objectives

8.   The developed contracting parties do not expect reciprocity for commitments made by them in trade negotiations to reduce or remove tariffs and other barriers to the trade of less-developed contracting parties.

BIBLIOGRAPHY

BOOKS AND ARTICLES

Anjaria, S. J. "The Multinational Trade Negotiations and Tariff Reduction." *Finance and Development.* 12, no. 4, (Dec. 1975): 25–28.

Arndt, S. W. "Customs Union and the Theory of Tariffs." *American Economic Review* 59, no. 1 (March 1969): 108–18.

———. "On Discriminatory versus Non-preferential Tariff Policies." *The Economic Journal* 78 (December 1968): 971–79.

Balassa, Bela. *The Theory of Economic Integration.* Homewood, Ill.: Richard D. Irwin, 1961.

———. "Towards a Theory of Economic Integration." *Kylos* 14, no. 1 (1961): 1–14.

———. "Trade Creation and Trade Diversion in the European Common Market." *The Economic Journal* LXXVII, no. 305 (March 1967): 1–21.

Baldwin, Robert E. *Non-Tariff Distortions of International Trade.* Washington: The Brookings Institution, 1970.

Balogh, Thomas. "Africa and the Common Market." *Journal of Common Market Studies* 1, no. 1 (1962): 79–112.

Barnes, W. G. *Europe and the Developing World. Association under Part IV of the Treaty of Rome.* European Series no. 2, Political and Economic Planning (PEP). Chatham House: London, 1967.

Bauer, P. T., and Ward, Barbara. *Two Views on Aid to Developing Countries.* London: Institute of Economic Affairs, Occasional Paper 9, 1970.

Blumenthal, W. Michael. "A World of Preferences." *Foreign Affairs* 48, no. 3 (April 1970): 549–60.

Brewster, Havelock and Thomas, Clive Y. "Aspects of the Theory of Economic Integration." *Journal of Common Market Studies* 8, no. 2 (December 1969): 110–32.

Byé, Maurice. "Customs Unions and National Interests." *International Economic Papers* 3 (London: Macmillan, 1953): 208–34. Translated from "Unions Douanières et Données Nationales," *Economie Appliquée* (January/March 1950).

Caves, Richard E., and Jones, Ronald W. *World Trade and Payments.* Boston: Little, Brown, 1973.

Coffey, Peter, and Presley, John R. *European Monetary Integration.* London: Macmillan, 1971.

Cooper, C. A., and Massell, B. F. "A New Look at Customs Union Theory." *The Economic Journal* 75 (1965): 742–47.

Cooper, Richard N. "The European Community's System of Generalized Tariff Preferences: A Critique." *Journal of Development Studies* 8, no. 4 (July 1972): 379–94.

Corbet, Hugh, ed. *Trade Strategy and the Asian-Pacific Region.* London: Allen and Unwin, 1970.

Cosgrove, Carol Ann. "The Common Market and its Colonial Heritage." *Journal of Contemporary History* 4, no. 1 (January 1969): 73–87.

————, and Twitchett, Kenneth, J. "The Second Yaounde Convention in Perspective." *International Relations* 3, no. 9 (May 1970): 679–89.

Curtis, Thomas B., and Vastine, John Robert, Jr. *The Kennedy Round and the Future of American Trade.* New York: Praeger, 1971.

Curzon, Gerard. *Multilateral Commercial Diplomacy.* London: Michael Joseph, 1965.

Curzon, Victoria. *The Essentials of Economic Integration, Lessons of EFTA Experience.* London: Macmillan, 1974.

Dam, Kenneth W. *The GATT Law and International Economic Organization.* Chicago: University of Chicago Press, 1970.

Denton, G. R., ed. *Economic Integration in Europe.* Reading University Studies on Contemporary Europe 3. London: Weidenfeld and Nicolson, 1969.

Doimi Di Delupis, Ingrid. *The East African Community and Common Market.* Development Text. London: Longmans, 1970.

Ellsworth, P. T. *International Economics.* New York: Macmillan, 1938.

————. *The International Economy. Theory and Practice from Mercantilism to the Formation of the EEC.* 3rd ed. New York: Macmillan, 1964.

European Community. September 1970, December 1971, September 1972, February 1973, June 1974, July/August 1974.

Evans, John W. *The Kennedy Round in American Trade Policy, The Twilight of the GATT?* Cambridge: Harvard University Press, 1971.

Everts, Ph. P., ed. *The European Community in the World.* Rotterdam: Rotterdam University Press, 1972. Proceedings of the Conference of the Institute for International Studies and the Europe Institute, University of Leyden: "The External Relations of the Enlarged European Community," May 1971.

Feld, Werner. *The European Common Market and the World.* Englewood Cliffs, N.J.: Prentice-Hall, 1967.

Findlay, Ronald. *Trade and Specialization.* Harmondsworth: Penguin, 1970.

Franck, T. M., and Weisband, E., eds. *A Free Trade Association.* London: University of London Press, 1968.

Giersch, Herbert. "Economic Union Between Nations and the Location of Industries." *Review of Economic Studies, 1949–50* 17(2), no. 43: 87–97.

Haberler, Gottfried von. *The Theory of International Trade with Its Application to Commercial Policy.* London: W. Hodge, 1933. (English translation, 1950.)

Hallett, Graham. *The Economics of Agricultural Policy.* Oxford: Blackwell, 1968.

Harrod, Roy, and Hague, D. C., eds. *International Trade Theory in a Developing World.* London: Macmillan, 1963. (Proceedings of a conference held by the International Economic Association, 1961.)

Helleiner, G. K. *International Trade and Economic Development.* Harmondsworth: Penguin, 1972.

Hinshaw, Randall. *The European Community and American Trade.* New York: Praeger, 1964.

Hodgson, Robert D. and Stoneman, Elvyn, A. *The Changing Map of Africa.* Princeton, N.J.: Van Nostrand, 1968.

Hoffman, Michael, L. Can the GATT System Survive? *Lloyds Bank Review* 73 (July 1964): 1–14.

Ingram, James C. *International Economic Problems.* 2d ed. New York: John Wiley and Sons, 1970.

International Monetary Fund, *IMF Survey, August 27, 1973.*

Jackson, John H. *World Trade and the Law of GATT* (A Legal Analysis of the General Agreement on Tariffs and Trade). New York: Bobbs-Merrill, 1969.

Johnson, D. Gale. *World Agriculture in Disarray.* London: Macmillan, 1973.

Johnson, H. G. *Economic Policies towards Less-developed Countries.* London: Allen and Unwin, 1967.

———. "The Economic Theory of Customs Union." *Pakistan Economic Journal* 10, no. 1 (March 1960):14–32.

———. "An Economic Theory of Protectionism, Tariff Bargaining, and the Formation of Customs Union." *Journal Political Economy* 73 (1965): 256–83.

————. "The Gains from Free Trade with Europe: An Estimate." *Manchester School* 26 (1958): 247–55.

————. *Money, Trade and Economic Growth.* London: Allen and Unwin, 1962.

————, ed. *New Trade Strategy for the World Economy.* London: Allen and Unwin, 1969.

————. "Trade Preferences and Developing Countries." *Lloyds Bank Review,* no. 80 (April 1969), pp. 1–18.

Jones, Edgar. "The Fund and UNCTAD." *Finance and Development* 8, no. 3 (September 1971): 29.

Kahnert, F., et al. *Economic Integration among Developing Countries.* Paris: Development Center of the Organization for Economic Cooperation and Development, 1969.

Kenen, P., and Lawrence, R. *The Open Economy.* New York: Columbia University Press, 1968.

Kindleberger, Charles, P. *International Economics.* 4th ed. Homewood, Ill.: Richard D. Irwin, 1968.

Knox, Francis. *The Common Market and World Agriculture. Trade Patterns in Temperate-zone Foodstuffs.* New York: Praeger, 1972.

Krauss, M. B., ed. *The Economics of Integration.* London: Allen and Unwin, 1973.

————. "Recent Developments in Customs Union Theory: An Interpretive Survey." *Journal of Economic Literature* 10, no. 2 (June 1972): 413–36.

Kravis, Irving B. " 'Availability' and Other Influences on the Commodity Composition of Trade." *The Journal of Political Economy* 64, no. 2 (April 1956): 143–55.

Kreinin, M. E. "Effects of Tariff Changes on Imports." *The American Economic Review* 51, no. 3 (June 1961):310–24.

————. "Effects of the EEC on Imports of Manufactures." *Economic Journal* 82, no. 327 (September 1972): 897–920.

Lawrence, R. "Primary Products, Preferences and Welfare: The EEC and Africa." In *International Economic Integration,* edited by P. Robson. Harmondsworth: Penguin, 1972.

Lipsey, R. G. "The Theory of Customs Unions: A General Survey." *The Economic Journal* 70, no. 279 (September 1960): 496–513.

————. "The Theory of Customs Unions: Trade Diversion and Welfare." *Economica* 24 (1957): 40–46.

Mally, Gerhard. *The European Community in Perspective: The New Europe, the United States and the World.* Lexington, Mass.: Lexington Books, 1973.

Matthews, J. "Free Trade and the Congo Basin Treaties." *South African Journal of Economics* 27, no. 4 (December 1959): 293–300.

———. "Prospect of an Association Agreement between South Africa and the EEC." *South African Journal of Economics* 38, no. 2 (June 1970): 152–62.

———. "Some Aspects of Common Market Trade with Africa." *South African Journal of Economics* 38, no. 1 (March 1970): 94–98.

Mayne, Richard. *The Recovery of Europe: From Devastation to Unity.* New York: Harper and Row, 1970.

Meade, J. E. *Trade and Welfare: The Theory of International Economic Policy* 2. London: Oxford University Press, 1955.

———. *The Theory of Customs Unions.* Amsterdam: North-Holland, 1955.

———, et al. *Case Studies in European Economic Union: The Mechanics of Integration.* Royal Institute of International Affairs. London: Oxford University Press, 1962.

Mikesell, R. F. "The Theory of Common Markets as Applied to Regional Arrangements among Developing Countries." In *International Trade Theory in a Developing World,* edited by R. F. Harrod and D. C. Hague.

Mundell, R. A. "Tariff Preferences and the Terms of Trade." *Manchester School of Economic and Social Studies* 32 (1964): 1–13.

Murray, Tracy. "How Helpful Is the Generalized System of Preferences to Developing Countries?" *The Economic Journal* 83, no. 330: 449–55.

Myint, H. "The 'Classical Theory' of International Trade and the Under-Developed Countries." *The Economic Journal* 68, no. 270 (June 1958): 317–37.

Ohlin, Bertil. Interregional and International Trade. Harvard Economic Studies 39. Cambridge: Harvard University Press, 1935.

Okigbo, P. N. C. *Africa and the Common Market.* London: Longmans, 1967.

Ouattara, Alassane D. "Trade Effects of the Association of African Countries with the European Economic Community." *I.M.F. Staff Papers* 20, no. 2 (July 1973): 499–543.

Overseas Development Institute. *ODI Briefing Paper: The Lomé Convention.* London: March 1975.

Patterson, Gardner. *Discrimination in International Trade, The Policy Issues 1945–1965.* Princeton: Princeton University Press, 1966.

———. "Would Tariff Preferences Help Economic Development?" *Lloyds Bank Review,* no. 76 (April 1965): 18–30.

Pincus, John A., ed. *Reshaping the World Economy: Rich Countries and Poor.* Englewood Cliffs, N.J.: Prentice-Hall, 1968.

————. Trade, Aid and Development: The Rich and Poor Nations. New York: McGraw-Hill, 1967.

Poincilit, Erhart. "Tariff Preferences for Developing Countries." *OECD Observer.* Organization for Economic Cooperation and Development. (February 1970): 3–7.

Robson, Peter. *Economic Integration in Africa.* London: Allen and Unwin, 1968.

————, ed. *International Economic Integration.* Harmondsworth: Penguin, 1972.

Scitovsky, T. *Economic Theory and Western European Integration.* Stanford: Stanford University Press, 1958.

Seers, Dudley, and Joy, Leonard. *Development in a Divided World.* Harmondsworth: Penguin, 1970.

Shibata, H. "The Theory of Economic Unions: A Comparative Analysis of Customs Unions, Free Trade Areas and Tax Unions. Sections 4 and 5 in C. in *Fiscal Harmonization in Common Markets* 1, edited by C. Shoup. New York: Columbia University Press, 1967.

Södersten, Bo. *International Economics.* London: Macmillan, 1971.

Soper, Tom. "European Trade with Africa." *African Affairs* 67, no. 267 (April 1968): pp.144–51.

Swann, Dennis. *The Economics of the Common Market.* 2d ed. Penguin Modern Economic Texts. Harmondsworth: Penguin, 1972.

The Economist. London, March 31, 1973.

Tinbergen, Jan. *International Economic Integration.* Amsterdam: Elsevier, 1954.

————. *International Economic Integration.* 2d rev. ed. Amsterdam: Elsevier, 1965.

Uri, Pierre, ed. *From Commonwealth to Common Market.* Harmondsworth: Penguin, 1968.

————. *Trade and Investment Policies for the Seventies: New Challenges for the Atlantic Area and Japan.* New York: Praeger, 1971.

Vanek, Jaroslav. *International Trade, Theory and Economic Policy.* Homewood, Ill.: Richard D. Irwin, 1962.

Viner, Jacob. *The Customs Union Issue.* New York: Carnegie Endowment for International Peace, 1950.

Wall, David. "EEC General Preferences: How Effective Will They Be?" *European Community,* January 1972, pp. 21–23.

————. "Problems with Preferences." *International Affairs* 47, no. 1 (January 1971): 87–99.

Walsh, A. E., and Paxton, John. *Into Europe: The Structure and Development of the Common Market.* 2d ed. London: Hutchinson, 1972.

Wilcox, Clair. *A Charter for World Trade.* New York: Macmillan, 1949.

Williams, J. J. *The Competitive Situation for South Africa.* South African Foreign Trade Organization (SAFTO), 1971.

Wright, C. J. A. "The Probable Effects of Britain's Entry into the EEC on the Economy of South Africa." *The South African Banker* 70, no. 2 (May 1973): 123–30.

Young, David. *International Economics.* London: Inter Text Books, 1969.

OFFICIAL PUBLICATIONS

European Economic Community
    Commission of the European Communities. Memorandum of the Commission to the Council on the Future Relations between the Community, the Present AAMS States and the Countries in Africa, the Caribbean, the Indian and Pacific Oceans. Referred to in Protocol No. 22 to the Act of Accession. Luxembourg, April 4, 1973. COM(73) 500/fin.
    EEC and the African Associated States. *The Convention of Association, May 1963.* Royal Institute of International Affairs, Oxford University Press.
    Foreign Trade, Monthly Statistics. Office statistique des Communautés Europénnes. Centre Louvigny, Luxembourg, 1972.
    Information statistiques sur l'évolution des échanges commerciaux des E.A.M.A., des Etats associés de l'Afrique de l'est et des pays du Commonwealth de structure comparable. Commission des Communautés, Brussels, June 1971.
    "Lomé Dossier." *The Courier.* Special Issue, no. 31 (March 1975). Brussels, Commission of the European Communities.
    The Signing of the Lomé Convention. Commission of the European Communities, Information: Development and Cooperation. 88/75.

Treaty Establishing the European Economic Community and Connected Documents. Secretariat of the Interim Committee for the Common Market and Euratom, Brussels, 1957.

Eurostat, Foreign Trade, Monthly Statistics, Special number 1958–74. Luxembourg, Statistical Office of the European Communities.

General Agreement on Tariffs and Trade
    Basic Instruments and Selected Documents, Eighth Supplement. Geneva, 1960.
    Basic Instruments and Selected Documents, Ninth Supplement. Geneva, 1961.
    Basic Instruments and Selected Documents, Eleventh Supplement. Geneva, 1963.
    GATT Activities in 1970/71. Geneva, 1972.
    Generalized Preferences. Notification by the United States. L/4299, February 13, 1976.
    Press Release, 1051. Address given by Mr. O. Long, Director-General of GATT. January 26, 1970.

Press Release, 1082. June 26, 1971.
Press Release, 1122. "The 1973 Multilateral Trade Negotiations: The Crucial Choices Ahead." Address by Mr. O. Long, Director-General of GATT to the Polytechnic Association, Oslo. May 3, 1973.
Press Release, 1176. March 8, 1976.
Trends in International Trade. A Report by a Panel of Experts. Geneva, October 1958. (The "Haberler Report.")

Republic of South Africa
Report of the Commission of Inquiry into the Export Trade of the Republic of South Africa. 2 vols. R.P. 69/72. Pretoria: Government Printer, 1972.

United Kingdom
Commonwealth Preference. British Information Services, R. 5155/69.
General Agreement on Tariffs and Trade, Part IV: Trade and Development. Statement of Policy with texts of Part IV and related documents. London, H.M.S.O., Cmnd. 2618, 1965.
The Future of the Commonwealth: A British View. The Report of a Conference held at Ditchley Park, Oxfordshire, at the invitation of the Commonwealth Relations Office in conjunction with the Ditchley Foundation, April 25–27, 1963. Rapporteur: Dr. T. P. Soper. London, H.M.S.O., 1963.
United Nations Conference on Trade and Employment, November 21, 1947 to March 24, 1948. *Final Act and Havana Charter for an International Trade Organization,* Cmd. 7375. London, H.M.S.O. 1948.

UNCTAD (United Nations Conference on Trade and Development)
TAD/INF/459(PREF). September 23, 1970.
TD/B/AC.5/34. Add. 1. September 19, 1970.
TD/B/AC.5/34. Add.5/Rev. 1. September 24, 1970.
Monthly Bulletin, no. 80. April 1973.

INDEX

JACQUELINE MATTHEWS completed her Ph.D. in 1975 at the University of Natal, Durban, where she is Senior Lecturer in the Department of Business Administration.

Born in Brussels, she graduated from the Universities of Louvain and the Witwatersrand, where she was awarded an M.A. for a thesis on the open-door policy in central Africa. Her interest in international economics focused on the European Economic Community, and in 1971 she went to the International Institute at the University of Nice and obtained a postgraduate diploma in EEC Studies.

Dr. Matthews has also lived in Britain, India, and Zaïre. She is married and has three sons.